The Places We Save

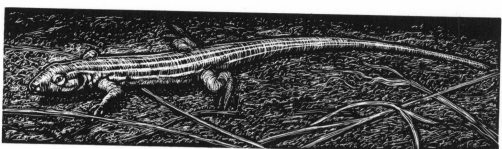

six-lined racerunner

Wisconsin Chapter of The Nature Conservancy

Dedicated to the members and volunteers
of the Wisconsin Chapter of The Nature
Conservancy who do so much to help save
the natural places of this state.

Written by Mary M. Maher
    Mixed Media / Madison, WI
Designed by Nancy E. Zucker
    Mixed Media / Madison, WI
Maps illustrated by Paul Kienitz
    Mixed Media / Madison, WI
Illustrated by Curt Carpenter
    Aspen, CO
Photography by Charles C. Mayhew III,
    R. Hamilton Smith & William R. Waldman
Cover Photo: R. Hamilton Smith

ISBN 0-9619854-0-2
5000 copies printed in February 1988.

Published by the Wisconsin Chapter of The Nature
Conservancy, 1045 East Dayton Street, Rm. 209,
Madison, Wisconsin 53703. (608) 251-8140.

Typeset by KC Graphics, Inc. / Madison, WI
Printed by Park Printing House / Verona, WI

Contents

coneflower

Our Natural Inheritance

Follow a path through the beauty of Wisconsin's protected prairies, woods and wetlands . . . the places we save.

tundra swan

There's a place in Sauk County where, in the middle of a summer's day, streaks of sunlight honeycomb through the lush canopy of treetops above a forest floor deeply covered in wood nettle and ferns. One of the only sounds heard in this peaceful setting is the song of the hooded warbler, a rare forest interior songbird. This place is *Baxter's Hollow*, a preserve for an endangered natural ecosystem—a deciduous forest watershed, a sanctuary of our natural inheritance. More than a dozen rare species and natural communities are safe in *Baxter's Hollow*, one of the many preserves owned and managed by the Wisconsin Chapter of The Nature Conservancy.

This book is a guide to those preserves. It includes individual descriptions of the biological communities protected by the Conservancy in Wisconsin and directions for finding each preserve. Most Conservancy preserves are open for careful public use as long as visitors honor the theme of preservation by enjoying these lands for passive recreation only—hiking, bird watching, nature study and photography. Preserves that contain plants and animals of scientific interest are often used for biological and ecological research. Sometimes a preserve remains closed to the public because a species or natural community under protection is at risk.

A History of Preservation

Like the national organization and other Nature Conservancy chapters, the Wisconsin Chapter is dedicated to preserving natural areas that represent a true diversity in plant and animal life. The Conservancy in Wisconsin concentrates in four program areas:

- ☐ **identification** of endangered natural community and species habitats;
- ☐ **protection** of those areas through purchase or other means;
- ☐ **stewardship** and management of protected areas;
- ☐ **development** of funding and support among individuals, corporations and foundations.

Since 1960, the Wisconsin Chapter of The Nature Conservancy has protected more than 22,000 acres of prairie, wetland and forest ecosystems that are scientifically noteworthy in this region, areas endangered by the impact of human development. Some acquisitions are transferred or sold to universities, museums, government agencies or other conservation groups who then oversee preservation and public use. Among the 95 preserves listed here, 32 sites are owned and managed solely by The Nature Conservancy and 63 are under other ownership but were protected with help from the Conservancy. The 32 Conservancy-owned preserves are described in detail along with 10 others, significant because the Conservancy had a hand in achieving their protection. The rest are listed more briefly. By the year 2000, the Wisconsin Chapter aims to help protect an additional 30,000 acres of the most critical natural habitat remaining in Wisconsin. Close cooperation between the Conservancy and other conservationists, both public and private, remains essential in achieving this goal.

The Quiet Conservationists

The Nature Conservancy movement started in 1917 within The Ecological Society of America. It was the inspiration of a group of botanists and zoologists concerned about the loss of natural lands they needed to conduct research and make collections. In 1951, two committees of the Society formally became The Nature Conservancy, beginning what is now one of the most active conservation organizations in the United States. The Conservancy owns and manages some 950 projects representing the world's largest private natural preserve system. This achievement was possible because of a single-minded determination to preserve the nation's heritage of natural diversity. The Nature Conservancy works diligently to identify the most endangered species and their habitats, then bids on the open market or through other means to protect the land for preservation and study. The grace and professionalism with which the Conservancy works have earned widespread respect, not only among government agencies and corporate and industrial America, but among dedicated conservationists as well. Throughout Conservancy history, concerned citizens from *all* sectors have come together to support the organization's mission of protecting significant natural areas from destruction.

In the 1970s, The Nature Conservancy established a national Natural Heritage Program of sophisticated data collection and retrieval. Rare plants, animals and their habitats are catalogued state-by-state, providing each Chapter with information about the most critical areas needing protection. The Heritage staff of the Wisconsin Department of Natural Resources (DNR) Bureau of Endangered Resources gathers data on sites throughout the state and helps the Conservancy make decisions about protecting new preserves and managing existing ones. A growing number of volunteer naturalists has been enlisted to support this program statewide.

The Nature Conservancy has over 300,000 members nationally, with more than 9,000 of them in Wisconsin. Many of these donors give time as well as money to the organization. They are the "hands-on" conservationists who assist in caretaking and stewardship duties on the preserves. Conservancy members serve on the Chapter's Board of Trustees and on volunteer stewardship committees across the state. Such firm individual dedication to the mission of preservation is yet another example of Wisconsin's rich natural heritage — the people and the land in harmony.

The complete list of current Conservancy preserves in Wisconsin is included in this Guide, along with brief descriptions of other natural areas the Wisconsin Chapter took part in protecting. The Nature Conservancy of Wisconsin welcomes your support and encourages you to enjoy and learn from these places we *all* work to save.

birch woods

Guidelines for Visiting Preserves

feather from a flicker

Each Wisconsin Conservancy preserve listing includes details about public access. The Conservancy requests visitors to respect the nature of the land at all times. Please observe rules about passive recreation — hiking, bird watching, nature study and photography ONLY in these protected areas. Because certain preserves are generally not open to the public, they are marked as **Special Access**. Contact the Conservancy office at 1045 E. Dayton St., Rm. 209, Madison, WI 53703 or call (608) 251-8140 for information about visiting these places.

Make the most of your visit to a Conservancy preserve by observing these guidelines:

☐ **Come Prepared** Wear comfortable footwear, suitable for hiking (see *Map Tips* below), but no heavy, cleated boots, please. Pack some rain gear and wear long pants with socks over them to protect yourself from ticks and poison ivy or poison sumac. Bring along sunscreen and insect repellant for protection. For a long hike, outfit yourself with a filled water bottle for thirst quenching. And, of course, remember your camera, binoculars, this Guide or other field guides and a compass.

☐ **Map Tips** Site maps included with the public-access preserves provide the key to getting around. Most distinct footpaths are marked but to help visitors anticipate hiking conditions for each preserve, we developed the following visual key:

1 shoe = level terrain, path usually present
2 shoes = uneven terrain, may be wet
           & rocky in spots
3 shoes = steady climb or uneven terrain
           for long distances
4 shoes = fairly strenuous, may be
           scrambling uphill or in wetland
Canoe = best way to travel is by water

NOTE: Wheelchairs possible on *1- or 2-shoe* preserves ONLY.

☐ **Preserve Our Preserves** Please DO NOT pick flowers, berries, nuts, mushrooms, shells, rocks or other parts of the natural landscape. Collecting flora, fauna and minerals is allowed for scientific research ONLY and requires a permit from the Wisconsin Conservancy office.

☐ **Respect These Restrictions** The following activities are NOT ALLOWED on Conservancy preserves:
- Pets (even on a leash, except seeing-eye dogs);
- Horseback riding;
- Bicycles or other off-road vehicles;
- Camping or picnic fires;
- Rock climbing or spelunking;
- Fishing or trapping;
- Hunting (except by permit from Wisconsin office of the Conservancy on preserves where deer damage is excessive);
- And, do not trespass on private property adjacent to Conservancy preserves.

Enjoy your visit and please report any vandalism or other problems you encounter to the Conservancy. For more information about The Nature Conservancy and the Wisconsin Chapter, contact our office at 1045 E. Dayton St., Rm. 209, Madison, WI 53703. (608) 251-8140.

What is a State Natural Area?

Many Wisconsin Conservancy preserves are listed here as either a *Dedicated* or *Designated State Natural Area*.

These are legal distinctions established by the Legislature of the State of Wisconsin to extend environmental protection over areas of land or water that remain largely undisturbed and are of significant educational or scientific value. *Dedication* or *Designation* may apply to both private and public lands. The term *Designated State Natural Area* is used to protect land through an exchange of agreements between landowners and the State of Wisconsin. *Designations* may be cancelled. Setting aside a *Dedicated State Natural Area* signifies a transfer of land or permanent conservation easement on the land to be held in trust for the people of Wisconsin. *Dedication* ensures protection of the land's natural values in perpetuity.

Wisconsin's
Natural Landscape

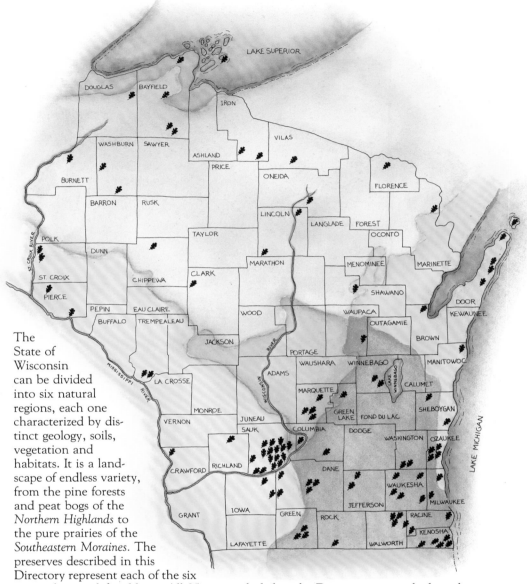

The State of Wisconsin can be divided into six natural regions, each one characterized by distinct geology, soils, vegetation and habitats. It is a landscape of endless variety, from the pine forests and peat bogs of the *Northern Highlands* to the pure prairies of the *Southeastern Moraines*. The preserves described in this Directory represent each of the six regional types defined here. All 95 sites included in the Directory are marked on the map and organized into three sections: (1) preserves the Conservancy owns and manages; (2) a sampling of preserves the Conservancy has played a role in protecting; and (3) a list of other sites the Conservancy has helped protect in Wisconsin. Preserves appear in alphabetical order within each section. Consult the *Index* at the back for specific locations by name.

☐ Lake Superior Boreal
- balsam fir & white spruce
- red clays & pink soils
- undulating to rolling plains
- peat extensive in some wetlands

☐ Northern Highlands
- maple, hemlock & yellow birch interrupted by extensive stands of white pine & red (Norway) pine
- peat bog with black spruce, tamarack & white cedar

☐ Western Driftless Upland
- hilly with little evidence of glaciation
- oak savanna, southern mesic forest
- pure prairie stands
- extensive river bottom forest

☐ Southeastern Moraines
- sequences of glaciated ridges & lowlands
- southern mesic forest, oak savanna
- pure prairie stands
- many wetland communities

☐ Lake Michigan Lowland
- American beech range in Wisconsin
- southern & northern mesic forest interspersed with wetland
- maple, hemlock, yellow birch & beech (northern)
- maple, basswood, elm & beech (southern)

☐ Central Sands Transition
- nearly level terrain with sandstone buttes
- oak savanna & pine barrens
- vast wetland communities
- soils feature sand, shallow peats & mucks

Baraboo River Floodplain Forest

white ash in winter

Precious woodland species thrive as though in another age, sheltered in a well-preserved river forest.

The flat, lush lowland that characterizes the Baraboo River Floodplain Forest is one of the few such habitats in the state that has gone undisturbed for decades. As a result, this Conservancy preserve contains a mature forest and a diverse high-quality understory of over 50 species. These were major reasons it was dedicated as a State Natural Area in 1985.

The flat terrain of the forest is crisscrossed by many sloughs or watery hollows that emphasize its proximity to running water. Flooding occurs yearly, a natural means by which to sustain the marsh and bog species here.

Among the tree species in full maturity in the forest are swamp maple, sugar maple, black ash and white ash. Ground layer species include woodbine, wood nettle, spotted jewel weed and whitegrass. There is also evidence of the rare hop-like sedge (*Carex lupuliformis*), a native prairie grass-like plant that survives only in a few mature river-bottom forests in Wisconsin.

The Nature Conservancy acquired the Baraboo River Floodplain Forest as a gift from previous owners Thomas and Luellen Ralston.

Protected: 22 Acres. Protection Goal: 26 Acres. Southcentral Wisconsin. Located along the Baraboo River in Columbia County. High-quality floodplain forest dedicated as a State Natural Area. Owned by The Nature Conservancy of Wisconsin and managed jointly by the Conservancy and the Wisconsin Department of Natural Resources. **Special Access Only.** Contact the Conservancy office at 1045 E. Dayton St., Rm. 209, Madison, WI 53703 for more information or call (608) 251-8140.

Bass Lake

northern Wisconsin pond

Wisconsin's northern wilderness is preserved in a land rich with lakes, tall pines and the timeless solitude of nature.

The namesake of this preserve is a pristine 15-acre soft water lake, the first northern wilderness lake The Nature Conservancy has taken under protection. Bass Lake serves as the centerpiece for the deeply forested site, located in the Northern Highland geographical region. This glaciated area contains the most extensive swamps and marshes (often called by their Chippewa name, *muskeg*) in the state.

Great diversity characterizes the vegetation at Bass Lake preserve. Sugar maple, red maple, yellow birch and white birch are there in a northern mesic forest type. The dry mesic forest is dominated by aspens and maples. In the swamp conifer forest rimming the Lake and other water bodies, mature tamarack and black spruce trees grow along with large white pines. Virtually undisturbed bogs, or *muskegs*, support additional shrubby vegetation such as the leatherleaf and bog laurel found here.

A wealth of shrubs and herbs make up the undergrowth throughout the preserve. Juneberry, alder-leaved buckthorn, raspberry and the American fly honeysuckle thrive here, along with pipewort, wild calla, sweet-scented bedstraw, sweet cicely, wild sarsaparilla and the unusual pitcher plant (*Sarracenia purpurea*).

Water is a major theme of the preserve. In addition to Bass Lake, a short stream and a portion of a second lake — both unnamed — are part of the landscape. Wildlife, such as the great blue heron, osprey and common loons, is found in abundance near these wetlands. Bald eagles and black bears have been spotted in the area and beaver dams have been found along the length of the stream.

The size and quality of the Bass Lake project represent a significant ecological preserve that encompasses a complete northern Wisconsin lake watershed. Conservancy biologists have identified several varieties of orchids, some of them rare. Since the Conservancy acquired the conservation easement on the land in 1982, valuable scientific work has been conducted by the Wisconsin Department of Natural Resources and other groups.

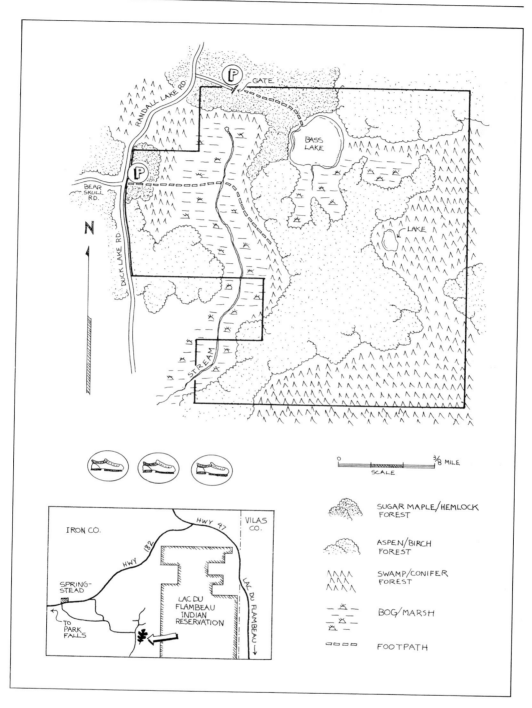

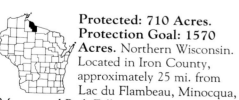

SUGAR MAPLE/HEMLOCK
FOREST

ASPEN/BIRCH
FOREST

SWAMP/CONIFER
FOREST

BOG/MARSH

FOOTPATH

**Protected: 710 Acres.
Protection Goal: 1570
Acres.** Northern Wisconsin.
Located in Iron County,
approximately 25 mi. from
Lac du Flambeau, Minocqua,
Mercer and Park Falls, west of Lac du
Flambeau Indian Reservation. Owned by
The Nature Conservancy through a gift
from the owner, who holds a life interest
on 10 acres and continues to manage the
entire parcel. Open to visitors for hiking
and observation.

Directions: From Park Falls, follow
Wisconsin Hwy. 182 east approx. 20 mi. to
Bearskull Rd.; travel southeast approx.
4 mi. to a "T" intersection with Randall
Lake Rd. and Duck Lake Rd. Park just east
of this intersection.

Baxter's Hollow/ R. D. & Linda Peters Preserve

Where the most endangered of birds find peaceful sanctuary, the sounds of forest and cold running stream mingle at the water's parting.

forest stream

Baxter's Hollow is one of the Wisconsin Chapter's largest, most impressive projects. Since 1969, the Conservancy has steadily acquired tracts of land in what is known as the Baraboo Bluffs area. Lush stands of trees and a mountain-like stream make Baxter's Hollow remarkable as one of the last remaining deep forest communities where a variety of wild species flourish. The current preserve contains southern Wisconsin's only undeveloped watershed. This is bordered by forest land where the numerous small streams that empty into Otter Creek originate.

The Creek is a central focus of Baxter's Hollow. It runs clear, soft and fast over quartzite bedrock boulders through a low gorge and is home to a rich collection of aquatic life rare in Wisconsin—such as the pickerel frog *(Rana palustris)* and at least five caddisfly species found in few other places.

Baxter's Hollow is a major part of the state's largest intact southern deciduous forest. Rugged stands of oak, hickory, maple and ash trees characterize the northern bluffs where quartzite outcroppings rise above the forest valley. Closer to the Creek, in what was once the Klondike Campground, alder thickets grow along the water's edge. Oak and hickory trees fill in beyond. One treasure of the Baxter's Hollow Preserve is the fact that despite limited human occupation of the area, the land has been left largely wild and untouched. Such conservation over the years has encouraged a natural community tally that includes many of the major vegetation types found in Wisconsin: shaded cliff, hemlock relic, northern dry-mesic (pine-hardwood) forest, southern dry-mesic (red oak) forest, southern mesic (maple-basswood) forest, sand barrens and others.

As many as 135 bird species have been recorded at Baxter's Hollow, considered one of the most important nesting areas for forest birds in southern Wisconsin. The Cooper's hawk, the broad-winged hawk and the worm-eating and hooded warbler are protected at Baxter's Hollow.

The geological face of Baxter's Hollow is a good example of the glaciated terrain common in this part of Wisconsin. Mineral deposits—flushed and compressed by ice flows and the waters of a pre-historic lake—formed the quartzite bedrock and sandstone cliffs apparent today. The highest point is 500 feet above the terrain. Rockshelters attributed to human use 10,000 to 20,000 years ago are seen at Baxter's Hollow and other parts of the Baraboo Bluffs, evidence of both Archaic and Woodland cultures.

Private landowners in the Baraboo Hills area have been important to the Conservancy's preservation of Baxter Hollow, making cooperative conservation of this critical bird and wildlife habitat a standard of their support.

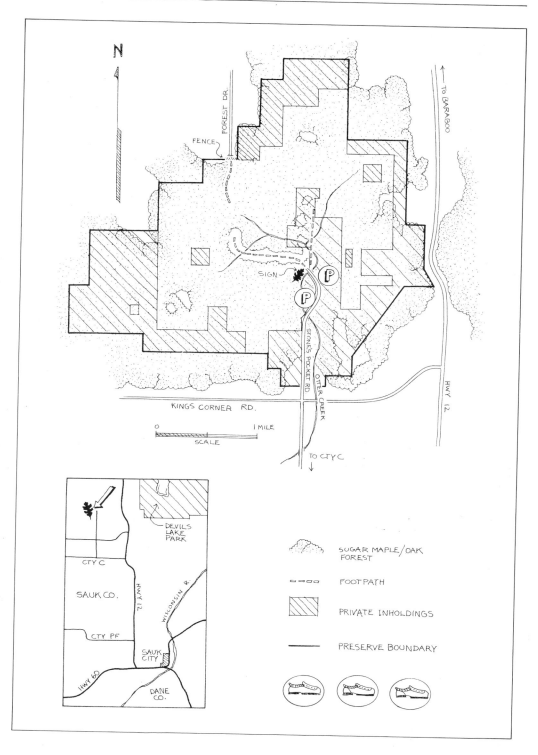

N

TO BARABOO

FOREST DR.

FENCE

SIGN

P

P

STONES POCKET RD.

OTTER CREEK

HWY 12

KINGS CORNER RD.

0   1 MILE
SCALE

TO CTY C

DEVILS LAKE PARK

CTY C

SAUK CO.

SAUK CITY

CTY PF

HWY 12

WISCONSIN R.

HWY 60

DANE CO.

SUGAR MAPLE/OAK FOREST

FOOT PATH

PRIVATE INHOLDINGS

PRESERVE BOUNDARY

Protected: 2900 Acres. Protection Goal: 3800 Acres. Southwestern Wisconsin. Located in Sauk County between Sauk City and Baraboo. Includes valuable watershed area with contiguous forest boundary. Dedicated as a Wisconsin Natural Area. Owned and managed by The Nature Conservancy of Wisconsin. Open to visitors for hiking and observa-tion. Some parcels of land within the Preserve remain private and visitors are reminded not to trespass.

Directions: From Sauk City, take US Hwy. 12 north for 8 mi. to Cty. C; take a left going west on C for 1-1/2 mi. to intersection with Stone's Pocket Rd.; turn right going north; drive 2 mi. into woods and park at one of several turn-off parking sites.

Black Earth Rettenmund Prairie

wood lily

A concentration of prairie plants is blended together in the rich brush strokes of nature on a tiny remnant of Wisconsin's past.

Black Earth Rettenmund Prairie is considered one of the few remaining examples of dry-mesic prairie in Wisconsin. This small, triangular tract of land—situated on the edge of a Dane County farm—sits serenely on a low knob and ridge, clearly visible from the road. A wide diversity of plant species survive here. More than 80 have been identified, some of them on the State list of threatened plants.

Among the rarest species existing on the Rettenmund Prairie are the round-stemmed false foxglove (*Gerardia gattingeri*) and Hill's thistle (*Cirsium hilli*). Shrubs, aspen and other young trees also grow along the ridge of the Prairie, once rated among the top ten natural areas of Dane County in private ownership. After it was acquired by the Conservancy in 1986, Black Earth Rettenmund Prairie was dedicated as a State Natural Area, insuring its continued protection.

Though there was some grazing on the land in the 1930s and evidence of a tractor path at one time, the prairie land has been preserved in recent years by brush removal and periodic burnings done by local volunteers. A strip of agricultural land on the northeast corner serves as a buffer from the roads that intersect there. Recordings of plant species began some years earlier when scientists from the University of Wisconsin conducted evaluations. The Rettenmund Prairie was once used by ecologist John Curtis for teaching and today the area continues to be used as a natural laboratory of rare and abundant flora.

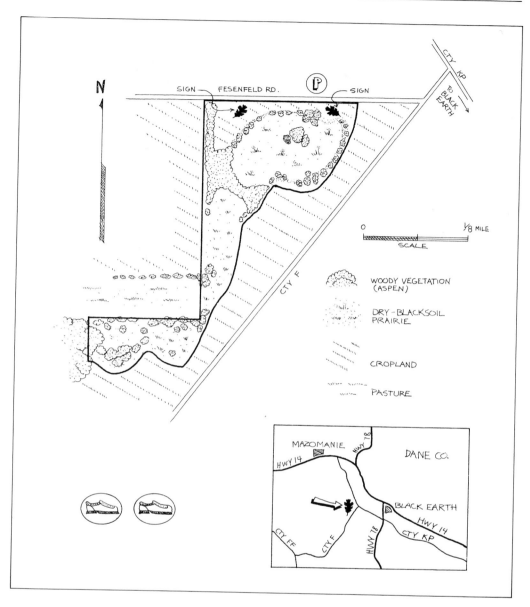

Protected: 17 Acres. Protection Goal: 17 Acres.
Southcentral Wisconsin. Located in Dane County, west of Black Earth. Dedicated as a State Natural Area. Owned by The Nature Conservancy of Wisconsin and managed jointly by the Conservancy and the Wisconsin Department of Natural Resources. Used extensively for education and open to visitors for prairie nature study.

Directions: Prairie lies in a triangle corner of a field southwest of the intersection of Fesenfeld Rd. and Cty. F. *From Black Earth,* travel west on Cty. KP (off Hwy. 78) for 1 mi., then south on Cty. F for 1/4 mi. to Fesenfeld Rd. and turn right. *From Mazomanie,* take Cty. KP south 2 mi.; turn right on Cty. F and travel 1/4 mi. to the Fesenfeld intersection. Park along the shoulder of Fesenfeld Rd., keeping your car 4 ft. clear of the road.

Chiwaukee Prairie

prairie thunderheads

Stand close to the lakeshore and you can see the old oaks rise above lush prairie plants and suburban intersections.

It has been described as a "primeval sanctuary" left in the wake of the glacier that passed through Wisconsin and the upper Midwest more than a million years ago. Now, Wisconsin's Chiwaukee Prairie is considered the last unbroken stretch of prairie of its kind in the state, home to more than 400 native plant species. And stretch it does. Encompassing a narrow run of shorefront along Lake Michigan, about four miles south of Kenosha, Chiwaukee Prairie sits like a strip of found treasure in the midst of limited urban and commercial development. Much of that development was arrested in 1965 when the Conservancy became involved in organized efforts to preserve this unique ecosystem. Today, Chiwaukee Prairie is protected as a National Natural Landmark and a State Natural Area.

Chiwaukee Prairie is characterized as a "beach ridge complex," a landscape alternating between low ridges and shallow swales left by the lake's retreat. This combination of sandy and clay soils gives Chiwaukee a rich and diverse vegetation that ranges from the savannah aspect of open-grown oaks to wet prairie plants in marshy shallows.

The inventory of plant species at Chiwaukee is of pre-eminent value. It is, in fact, one of the richest preserves in the nation for a diversity of rare types, among them the endangered prairie white-fringed orchid (*Platanthera leucophaea*). Chiwaukee contains the largest concentration of this prairie flower in the Midwest. The rare pink milkwort, smooth phlox, prairie Indian plantain, chestnut sedge and prairie sand coreopsis all thrive in this natural setting along with fragrant prairie grasses swaying softly against the horizon.

Many seasons of nature work their mastery at Chiwaukee Prairie: shooting stars, prairie violets and wood betony bloom in the spring; acres of goldenrod, asters and gentians appear in autumn. The colors and scents of Chiwaukee's nature settle comfortably here, where sweeping prairie stands as a backdrop to Lake Michigan.

Chiwaukee Prairie is also home to a variety of wildlife. Kit foxes, white-tailed deer, raccoons, ground squirrels and woodchucks roam the dry prairie ridges. Among some 76 bird species recorded, the upland sandpiper, king rail, marsh wrens and the eastern meadowlark are protected at Chiwaukee. Numerous reptiles, amphibians and small mammals are found in abundance where the lush prairie vegetation goes to the swales—the shallow, wet prairie habitat that is an enduring feature of Chiwaukee.

Early Indian occupation of the site is apparent on the sand ridge to the west of Chiwaukee. There, chert flakes, scrapers, hunting points and spears of Woodland and Upper Mississippi culture have been unearthed.

Considered unique in Wisconsin, there is no comparable area throughout the region. A fortunate history of protection and its large size make it possible to preserve species diversity and high community integrity at Chiwaukee Prairie.

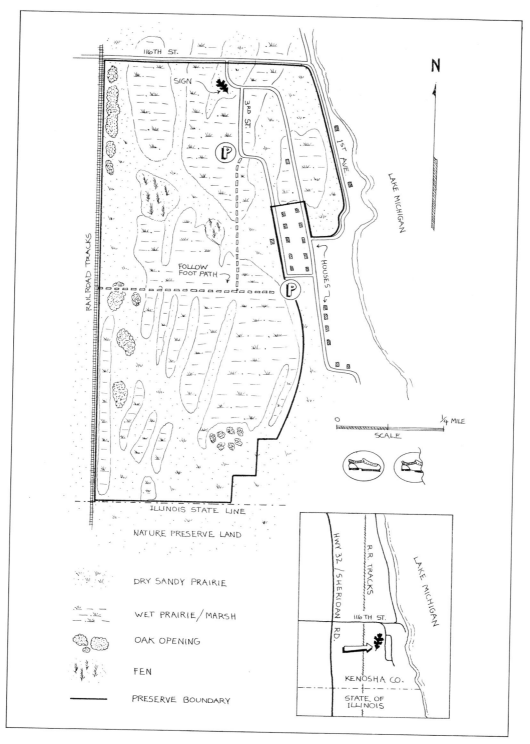

Protected: 165 Acres. Protection Goal: 260 Acres. Southeastern Wisconsin. Located in the Town of Pleasant Prairie in southeast Kenosha County. Bordered on the south by the Wisconsin/Illinois state line, on the east by Lake Michigan. Owned and managed by The Nature Conservancy of Wisconsin and the University of Wisconsin-Parkside.

Frequently used for educational studies and field trips. Open to visitors for hiking and observation.

Directions: Take Hwy. 50 exit off I-94; go east on Hwy. 50 for 6-1/4 mi. to Sheridan Rd. (Hwy. 32); then south 4 mi. to Tobin Rd. (116th St.); take Tobin Rd. east for 3/4 mi. to first right turn past railroad tracks; large sign marks entry 1/2 block down.

Decorah Mounds

Rolling prairieland cut through with rich forest . . . the Wisconsin landscape as the first settlers must have seen it.

badger

Decorah Mounds is a classic Mississippi River bluff that provides a commanding view of the river valley and surrounding farmland. Mixed hardwood forest and dry prairie are combined here beneath the sweep of a vertical limestone cliff — 1200 ft. above sea level at its highest point. The Nature Conservancy received Decorah Mounds as a gift from Harlan and Verneille Hunter, who farm the adjacent land. The first 30-acre parcel was donated in 1976 and an additional 10 contiguous acres added in 1986.

Decorah Mounds is in the driftless, or unglaciated, area of west central Wisconsin where the land is characterized by greatly dissected uplands and lowlands covered with deep sediment from river flow. Though the predominant vegetation at Decorah is dry oak forest, the site is significant because of the high-quality dry prairie remnant at the top of the mound.

Prairie land once covered the entire south and east slopes. Now, Decorah Mounds is one of few such sites remaining in western Wisconsin, where most of the prairie has been lost to agriculture and forest. Since acquiring the preserve, the Conservancy has been working to restore this dry prairie from the small patch that existed in 1976. Overgrowth of sweet clover and aspen were threatening prairie plant species such as bluestem grasses, leadplant, puccoon, pasque flower and butterfly weed. More frequent, controlled burnings of overgrowth and dead grasses continue to help spark a renewal of the Decorah prairie.

The forest at Decorah Mounds grades from large open-grown oaks with a dense understory of brush and blackberries to a more mesic, even-aged stand with ferns and showy orchids. Underbrush on the north slope is dominated by round-leaved dogwood and an abundance of young basswood. Shooting stars, trilliums and Dutchman's breeches have been found in the woods.

North of the prairie site, a vertical limestone cliff stands about ten feet high, composed of bare rock except for crevices where columbine and polypody fern are found growing. The white camas (*Zigadenus elegans*) prairie plant can be found at the top along the west boundary, its beauty matching the scenic vista from this point.

Wildlife thrives in Decorah Mounds. Animals sighted here include white-tailed deer, fox, turkey vulture, rose-breasted grosbeak, red-bellied woodpecker and indigo bunting.

Recorded Decorah Mounds' history goes back more than a century and a half to the time when Winnebago Chief Decorah led a band of Indians against a threat from the Chippewa tribe. An old wagon road, built in the 1880s to connect the Decorah prairie to Galesville and points east, still defines one boundary of the site though the road was abandoned some 90 years ago. The east slope was logged prior to 1925 and the north mound logged some in the late 1930s and 1940s. The entire area was used as grazing land until about 1950. Previous owner Harlan Hunter grew up on this land and wanted to see it safe from destruction. When he and his wife made a gift of the land to the Conservancy, they maintained their personal interest in Decorah Mounds by sitting on the local committee that watches over the site, continuing to welcome visitors and answer their questions.

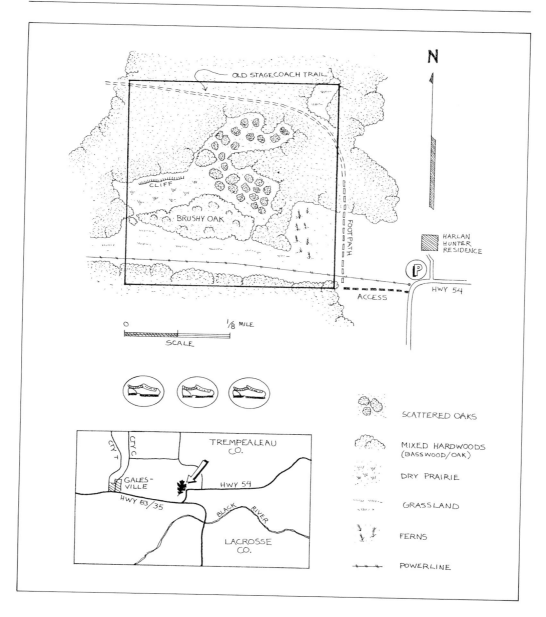

Protected: 40 Acres. Protection Goal: 40 Acres.
West Central Wisconsin. Located 2 miles east of Galesville in Trempealeau County. River bluff and prairie opening are along the western edge of Hunter's farm. Owned and managed by The Nature Conservancy of Wisconsin. Open to visitors for hiking and observation. Information available at the farmhouse.

Directions: Travel southeast from Galesville on Hwy. 54-35 to Hwy. 54; go north on Hwy. 54 for 1/2 mi. to a sharp corner where road heads east; park in the driveway or just off driveway of Harlan Hunter. Access is through the Hunter's farm. Please call ahead: (608) 582-2307.

Durst Rockshelter

More than a hint of early civilizations and the natural landscape they inhabited are apparent here, where rolling farmland turns to rugged rock and woodland.

rattlesnake

Picture outcroppings of vertical cliffs, some rising to 50 feet. In the south corner stands a sheer facing of sandstone shaded by a cantilevered overhang — giving the clear impression of a shelter. Forests of mature trees surround and fill the scene as pasture land and cultivated fields softly border the preserve on all sides. It is like a mirror image of the Wisconsin landscape, past and present together.

For this reason, Durst Rockshelter and the woods surrounding it have been under scientific scrutiny since 1954 when the State Archaeological Department began excavation work. Louis Durst owned the land during that time and gave his name to the site. Evidence of settlements by Archaic Indians more than 7000 years ago were unearthed during early digs and the cantilevered rockshelter formation is attributed to their use. Ceramic and arrowhead artifacts have been recovered over the years, indicating the existence of Middle and Late Woodland cultures.

Durst Rockshelter is one of the most significant archaeological sites in Wisconsin and, as such, is protected from development. The Wisconsin Conservancy acquired the land in 1965 from later owners Wilbert and Vera Neuman for the primary purpose of extending that protection. Secondary,

but essential to the Conservancy in acquiring the site, is the biological significance of the southern mesic and shaded cliff communities found here. A sandstone ridge runs east to west through the center of the preserve, establishing the rugged, glaciated look common to this southwestern Wisconsin area. Good quality mesic forest covers a third of the property, where mature sugar maples, basswood and red oak trees dominate. Northern mesic forest is found on the north slope. Yellow birch, basswood and sugar and red maples form a canopy in the ravine below; white oak and ironwood grow along the ridge tops. Ground cover includes Adam & Eve orchid, showy orchis, yellow lady-slipper, rattlesnake plantain, star flower, large-leaf aster and the rare three-bird orchid. A subarctic club moss is found on the north-facing slope.

Because it continues to be used as an archaeological site, Durst Rockshelter is not open to the public. Anyone wishing to make a limited hike through this area must contact The Nature Conservancy office for permission.

Protected: 40 Acres. Protection Goal: 40 Acres. Southwestern Wisconsin. Located in Sauk County near Leland, Wisconsin. Site of ongoing archaeological dig. Owned and managed by The Nature Conservancy of Wisconsin. **Special Access Only.** Contact the Conservancy office at 1045 E. Dayton St., Rm. 209, Madison, WI 53703 for more information or call (608) 251-8140.

Fairy Chasm

Imagine that a single step takes you from the city into a world where careful conservation protects an abundance of plants and wildlife.

great horned owl

Something magical seems to encircle the Fairy Chasm preserve—a remnant of coniferous forest that survives in an urban setting. There is an ethereal feeling here, where deep forest mingles with the crisp sound of water spilling over rocks. The last of the forests that covered this part of Wisconsin some 9000 years ago, this area has been closely studied since the first visits by Wisconsin's pioneering naturalists in the 1800s. Professional botanists and plant hobbyists have identified an array of species, many of them rare, growing as though in another time, another place.

Fairy Chasm is a wooded retreat in the city, only minutes from Milwaukee's downtown. A deep chasm cuts through the clay bluffs of Lake Michigan, carrying a stream of water from a network of smaller streams into the Lake. A northern forest of white pine, white cedar, yellow birch and beech grows on the north slope, a drier southern hardwood forest on the south slope.

The ravine that once framed open farm fields is now wild backyard to nearby homes. It is thanks, in large part, to the residents of the area that the Fairy Chasm was marked for protection almost a century ago. Before then, this bit of "unspoiled original landscape of Wisconsin" withstood destructive fires, pasturing and logging. But by 1893, the land was left to self-restoration and the forest grew lush again. During that same period, a resort community of lake homes was established *around* Fairy Chasm, leaving the unique ravine and bluff area to nature. Conservancy ownership opened Fairy Chasm to the public in 1970 and it is now a valuable outdoor laboratory for the study of rare plants and animals native to this habitat.

Fairy Chasm is haven to a lush collection of plants, including pinedrops (*Pterospora andromedea*), considered nearly extinct in Wisconsin. The white-fruited form of the red baneberry (*Actaea alba*) and the red-fruited form of the white baneberry (*A. rubra*), both uncommon in Wisconsin, are also found at Fairy Chasm. The setting is the key to their survival—forest shade with cool, running water into Lake Michigan.

The ravine and wooded bluffs are also home to native mammals, among them opossum, meadow vole, gray fox, mink, cottontail rabbit, woodchuck and occasional raccoon. The whole Chasm is an excellent and quite natural bird sanctuary.

Protected: 19 Acres. Protection Goal: 19 Acres. Southeastern Wisconsin. In the City of Mequon, south east tip of Ozaukee County. 20 minutes from downtown Milwaukee. Woods and bluff are a Scientific Study Area used for research and education. Owned and managed by The Nature Conservancy of Wisconsin. **Special Access Only.** Apply for access by contacting the Conservancy office at 1045 E. Dayton St., Rm. 209, Madison, WI 53703. (608) 251-8140.

Falk Woods

After more than a century of rapid urban growth all around, this haven of wood and fen remains in quiet isolation.

aspen woods

The boundaries of this preserve encompass two separate gifts made to the Conservancy over a decade. The first 58 acres, donated in 1973 by Henry Falk, is a fine forest upland-bog area with great diversity of native soils and vegetation. The second tract, added with a 1980 gift, contains a large fen and tamarack swamp where some species of rare plants are found, among them Ohio goldenrod (*Solidago ohioensis*). The entire parcel is remarkable for the fact it has escaped significant development despite close proximity to cities and major highways.

Another notable aspect of the Falk Woods preserve is a long history as a site for scientific study. Many naturalists, students and birding groups use this place as an outdoor laboratory. Abundant flora and fauna found here are becoming increasingly rare in this highly populated area of the state. Groups from UW-Milwaukee, Carroll College and the UW-Waukesha have conducted extensive ecological research at Falk Woods. Area birding groups also maintain a census of bird species.

The southern boundary of Falk Woods is formed by a glacial ridge, or esker. On the steep north face of this distinctive landmark, a dry-mesic forest grows, in transition from the oak remnants of a southern mesic forest. Large red oaks, shagbark hickory, white ash, ironwood and sugar maple trees — all characteristic of the dry-mesic transition — have emerged here. The selective logging and pasturing that occured before 1950 may have sparked some of the vegetational change.

From the forest, the land slopes to lowland vegetation such as sedges, aspen thickets and shrub-fen. This area is also scattered with elms and black ash trees. A tamarack swamp, dominated by shrubby cinquefoil (*Potentilla fruticosa*), is found north of Red-wing Creek, in what may have once been an ancient glacial lake. The springs and seeps from the swamp area feed into the Redwing, flowing east to west through the center of the preserve. Deer, fox, skunk, raccoon, cottontail rabbit and many other wildlife are found in Falk Woods. The diversity of trees and vegetation attracts a wide variety of birds and this preserve is an important nesting place in southeastern Wisconsin. Among species recorded with territories at Falk Woods are great-crested flycatcher, wood thrush, scarlet tanager, ovenbird, blue-winged warbler, veery and the black-and-white warbler.

The Conservancy protects this land primarily because of its potential for research and teaching in a diverse and relatively undisturbed ecosystem. Falk Woods continues to serve this purpose at the same time it remains a popular bird habitat and nature preserve.

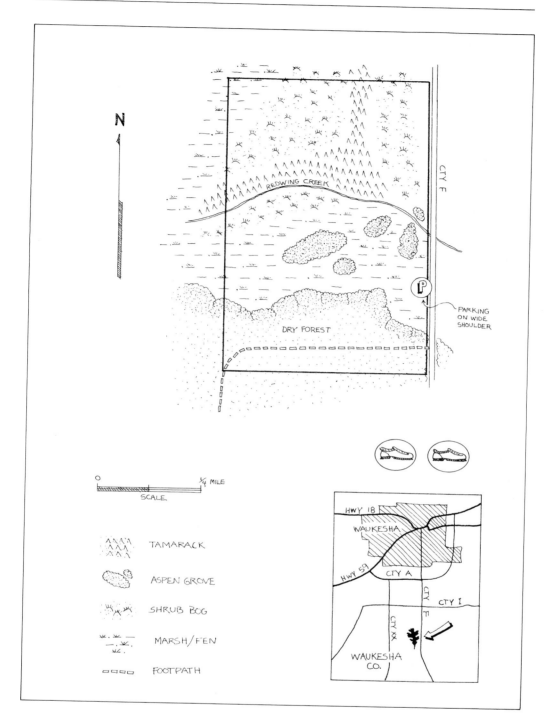

N

REDWING CREEK

CTY F

PARKING
ON WIDE
SHOULDER

DRY FOREST

0   ¼ MILE
SCALE.

TAMARACK

ASPEN GROVE

SHRUB BOG

MARSH/FEN

FOOTPATH

HWY 18
WAUKESHA
HWY 59   CTY A
CTY I
CTY F
CTY XX
WAUKESHA
CO.

**Protected: 113 Acres.
Preservation Goal: 113
Acres.** Southeastern
Wisconsin. Located in
Waukesha County, 4 mi.
south of the city of
Waukesha. Important site for scientific
study of a highly diverse ecosystem. Owned
by The Nature Conservancy of Wisconsin.
Managed by the Conservancy and the
Waukesha County Parks Department.
Open primarily for educational and
research purposes. Those wishing to use the
preserve must apply to the steward for permission. Contact the Conservancy office at
1045 E. Dayton St., Rm. 209, Madison, WI
53703 for information or call (608)
251-8140.

Directions: Travel south on Cty. Hwy. F
(Chinook Pass) approx. 4 mi. from
Waukesha. The preserve extends west from
F about 1/2 mi. south of Glendale Rd.

Gasser Sand Barrens

winter fields

Mounds of false heather and a stand of black oak lay the groundwork for a small prairie jewel set along a quiet country road.

The Gasser Sand Barrens is a real rarity in Wisconsin. Here, on just three acres of sandy land, a collection of more than 65 prairie and sand barrens plants thrives relatively undisturbed. Among them are "pioneer plants," annual, ephemeral species that act as forerunners and conditioners of the soil before sand prairie plants are established. Deep red poppy mallow (*Callirhoe triangulata*), a plant rare in Wisconsin, and the annual dwarf dandelion (*Krigia virginica*) are also found here.

The Barrens is located on an old Wisconsin River terrace on the eastern border of Wisconsin's driftless, or unglaciated, area. The lightly rolling and creviced terrain was formed by the effects of glacial outwash. A six-foot gully or erosion channel runs down the center of the rectangle and drains toward Honey Creek. The most significant pioneer plants are found on the slopes of this gully. A "sand blow" area exists, deeply covered in false heather (*Hudsonia tomentosa*).

Other plants found in abundance throughout the Barrens include Venus' looking glass, purple toadflax, wild roses, rock sandwort, American pennyroyal and small skullcap. A scattering of tall red cedars and a grove of black oak and bur oak trees are seen here. Rows of red pine trees border the south and west edges of the preserve,

planted over 15 years ago as a windbreak. The land was last part of a farm in 1930 and has been left to nature since.

Nine species of birds have been spotted in the Barrens, including the common bobwhite, the mourning dove, the whip-poorwill and the rufous-sided towhee. The preserve is so small, birders can enjoy their pastime from the roadside.

The Nature Conservancy acquired the preserve in 1969, a gift from the Gasser family who has farmed the adjacent land for over 100 years. Located just 30 miles from Madison, the Barrens have long been a popular outdoor laboratory for study by University naturalists. The educational potential of such a compact and rich preserve continues to be its primary appeal for conservation.

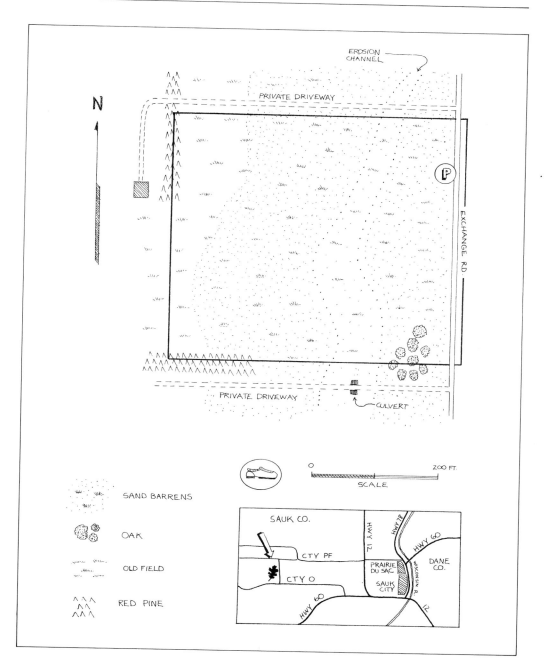

SAND BARRENS

OAK

OLD FIELD

RED PINE

SCALE

Protected: 3 Acres. Protection Goal: 3 Acres. Southwestern Wisconsin. Located in Sauk County west of Prairie du Sac and northeast of Honey Creek. Owned and managed by The Nature Conservancy of Wisconsin. Used extensively as a demonstration/study area. Birds on the preserve can be viewed from the roadside.

Directions: Travel west from Prairie du Sac on County PF for 3 to 4 mi. where PF turns north and Prairie Road continues straight west; follow Prairie Road west 3/4 mi. to Exchange Road; turn left and travel 1/2 mi. to preserve on right.

Hemlock Draw

Cool undergrowth accents the majesty of sandstone cliffs and a Wisconsin forest that protects birds both rare and common.

mushrooms

Hemlock Draw represents one of the Wisconsin Nature Conservancy's greatest moments. It is among the Chapter's earliest acquisitions in the Baraboo Hills, purchased in 1964 and originally conceived as a forest study area for the University of Wisconsin–Madison Botany Department. It is now a major preserve in the unglaciated portion of this region of southwestern Wisconsin. The size of the preserve has grown during nearly two decades of land purchase and donation and now includes a rocky canyon with clear-flowing stream, abundant woods and an area of abandoned fields returning to native plant life. Hemlock Draw is the protected habitat for several rare plants, including a sedge *(Carex prasina)* and, on the cliff, a saxifrage *(Sullivantia renifolia)*. The worm-eating warbler *(Helmitheros vermivores)* is one of several rare birds protected here.

As many as 11 types of distinct vegetative communities exist at Hemlock Draw. Once-active grazing land along the northern boundary gives way to a southern xeric forest and, eventually, to the dense stands of hemlocks that give this preserve its name. Geological formations of sedimentary rock exposed throughout the preserve stand as proof that this section of the Baraboo

Hills was a chain of sea islands in the Cambrian-Ordovician periods, some 500 million years ago.

The dolomite, or limestone-like ground rock, found along the north uplands and various sandstone types found in the southwestern corner are a product of this era. Below them is the much older Baraboo quartzite found at two locations, most significantly in one of the finest geologic features on the site — a narrow pillar of rock deposits called a "sea stack." A cliff area near the west boundary contains conglomerate with boulders up to 20 feet in length.

High-quality white oak, ironwood, American elm, bigtooth aspen and red oak trees are found where southern xeric forest is established here. Spreading hemlock groves prosper along the bluffs surrounding the gorge running east to west near the center of the preserve. Hemlock Draw also contains northern forest plants rare in this community such as the trailing arbutus *(Epigaea repens)*. Ground-layer plants and shrubs vary from sedges and skunk cabbage along flat areas to stands of ash species and witch hazel along the stream bottom. Ground cover at Hemlock Draw is rich in many native species, among them wood anemone, wild geranium, early meadow rue and lousewort. Because this site was spared the grinding effects of the last glacier, many plant species found here are relics of the glacial age when the edge of the towering ice mass was but a few miles to the north and east.

Hemlock Draw provides habitat for over 60 species of breeding birds, including barred owls, ruffed grouse, woodthrush, chickadee, five species of warblers and four species of woodpeckers.

The scientific and educational value of Hemlock Draw is unprecedented, thanks to the co-existence of so many diverse biotic communities on one site. The fact that both northern and southern communities and species thrive in such a small area continues to set Hemlock Draw apart among neighboring southwestern preserves.

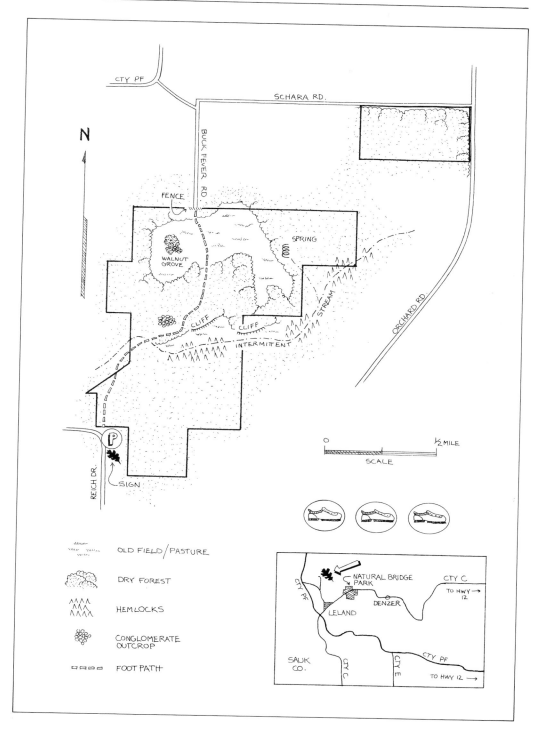

OLD FIELD/PASTURE

DRY FOREST

HEMLOCKS

CONGLOMERATE
OUTCROP

FOOT PATH

**Protected: 533 Acres.
Protection Goal: 700
Acres.** Southwestern
Wisconsin. Located in the
Baraboo Hills region of Sauk
County, in the Town of
Honey Creek and near Leland. Owned and
managed by The Nature Conservancy of
Wisconsin. Used extensively for research
and study. Open to visitors for nature
walks and wildlife observation.

Directions: Travel US Hwy. 12 northwest
of Sauk City for 2-1/2 mi. to the intersection with Cty. PF; travel west on PF for
12 mi. to Cty. C, turn right (NE) to Leland
(1/4 mi.); then turn left on Hemlock Rd. in
Leland to reach Reich Dr.; travel north on
Reich for approx. 1/2 mi. to reach preserve
entrance.

Hoganson Preserve

Sandhill cranes on the wing and a chorus of frogs may greet visitors to this sanctuary, part of Wisconsin's wetland heritage.

great blue heron

Hoganson Preserve presents the picture of a luxurious wetland landscape against the buffer of upland meadows. It is in such a setting that several threatened elements of nature have found safe habitat. Blanding's turtle (*Emydoidea blandingi*) and a yellow-throated marsh turtle have been recorded in the farm pond located in the south end of the preserve. Southern sedge meadow and fen, both state-threatened communities, are also found here.

A variety of streams flow in and out of the Hoganson tract. The most important of these is Sugar Creek, which feeds into the marsh area from the western edge of the preserve. Sugar Creek is considered the second-highest quality stream in southeastern Wisconsin.

Because this wetland area has been left in a relatively undisturbed, natural state and is contiguous to a wildlife management area managed by the Wisconsin Department of Natural Resources, Hoganson Preserve also serves as a sanctuary for the only major population of white-tailed deer in a three-county area and is an important nesting site for sandhill cranes. Other bird and animal species found here include the great blue heron, wood duck, barn swallow, leopard frog, American toad, muskrat and woodchuck.

The wetland tract east of the road contains a selection of marsh grasses and plants such as Canada bluejoint grass. Cattail patches and sedge stands are found throughout the marsh area. Native woodland areas are also part of the Hoganson Preserve. Oak openings run northwest along the bluffs over Sugar Creek and near the marsh. Ongoing rehabilitation of these areas by Conservancy volunteers and staff is done to reduce the density of invading Kentucky blue grass, sumac and buckthorn in favor of the oak woods.

The first 192 acres of Hoganson Preserve were presented as a gift to the Conservancy in 1984 by Les and Jane Hoganson, who made an additional gift of 27 acres in 1986.

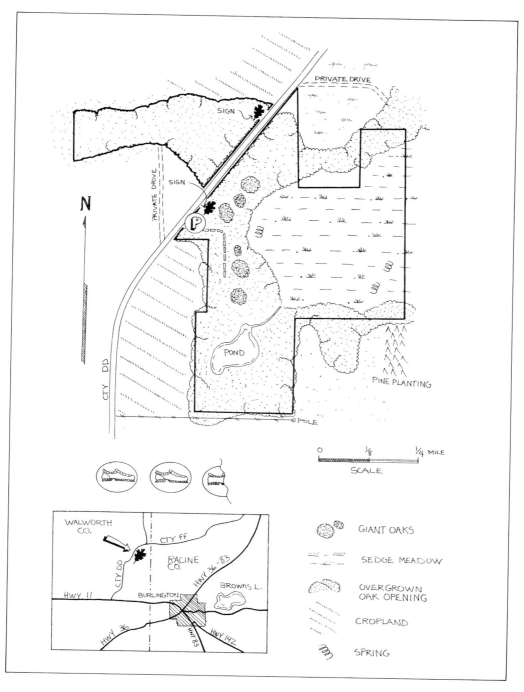

Protected: 219 Acres. Protection Goal: 250 Acres. Southeastern Wisconsin. Located in Walworth County in Spring Prairie Township northwest of Burlington, the preserve is part of the Honey Creek wetland complex. Owned and managed by The Nature Conservancy of Wisconsin. The preserve is intersected by County Highway DD. Open to visitors for hiking and observation.

Directions: Travel west from Burlington on Hwy. 11, then north for approx. 2 mi. on Cty. Hwy. DD. Though the preserve extends on both sides of the road, visitors are restricted to the section on the east side.

Holmboe Conifer Forest

Thick green in summer, a blend of rich golden hues in autumn, in every season wild brush and tall trees hug the river's edge.

pine grosbeak

I t is a familiar picture to anyone who has traveled the rural roads of northern Wisconsin—majestic pine trees growing deep alongside abundant maple, aspen and birch. Underneath runs a network of upriver streams and tributaries that feed the Wisconsin River. The forest floor is a cool greenhouse of sedges and forest marsh plants. Holmboe Conifer Forest is the essence of such a natural woodland, able to support a wide range of tree species, ground cover and soil types. The peace of nature abides here where more than 23 bird species find refuge.

The predominant features of the Holmboe preserve are the rolling contours of swamp and uplands, punctuated by the glacial *esker*, or gravel ridge, that runs along the southern boundary. The soil mix of alluvium or river sediment, marsh, loam and sand supports a rich ecosystem, most notably the trees of Holmboe — an abundant collection. White and red pine grow on the south ridges. In the swamps between ridges, tamarack and a good example of white cedar in isolated stands have taken hold. Swamp hardwoods at Holmboe include yellow birch, black ash and alder. On the northern slopes, hemlock and fir trees abound and on the west side — where gravel diggings were once done — some trembling aspen grow. One of the rarest of trees in Wisconsin is found at Holmboe, the yew. Good stands are often lost to deer browsing in the area.

Along the forest floor, prince's pine, three species of ground pine, barren strawberry, Pennsylvania sedge, labrador tea, pink lady-slipper and many other lowland species are in evidence. Seeping springs on the preserve drain into the Pelican River and provide the necessary moisture for the cedar vegetation of Holmboe and adjacent land.

The Holmboe Conifer Forest has been designated a Wildlife Sanctuary, a fact that ensures no disturbance and makes it possible for a sizable bird community to thrive. Species observed include the green heron, spotted sandpiper, least flycatcher, wood pewee, purple martin, hermit thrush, veery and the red-eyed vireo.

The Holmboe Conifer Forest was donated to the Conservancy by Frithjof Holmboe and his son, Thorvald. The Conservancy assumed full ownership and management of the preserve in 1965. Except for foot trails, there has been little disturbance to the land since logging days in the early part of the century. Remains of shanties were found along the ridge near the river where there was said to be a "hobo jungle" during the 1930s. The Holmboe preserve was designated a State Natural Area in 1969 and is often used for educational purposes.

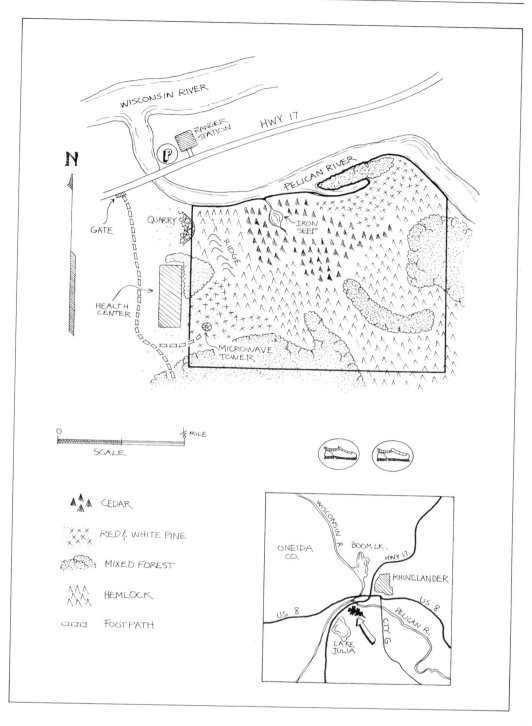

WISCONSIN RIVER

HWY 17

RANGER STATION

N

PELICAN RIVER

GATE

QUARRY

IRON SEEP

RIDGE

HEALTH CENTER

MICROWAVE TOWER

0   ⅛ MILE

SCALE

CEDAR

RED & WHITE PINE

MIXED FOREST

HEMLOCK

FOOT PATH

WISCONSIN R.

ONEIDA CO.

BOOM LK.

HWY 17

RHINELANDER

US 8

US 8

PELICAN R.

CTY G

LAKE JULIA

Protected: 32 Acres. Protection Goal: 32 Acres.
Northern Wisconsin. Located in Oneida County near Rhinelander, on the south bank of the Pelican River. Designated a State Natural Area and Wildlife Sanctuary by the Wisconsin Department of Natural Resources. Owned and managed by The Nature Conservancy of Wisconsin. Open to visitors for hiking and wildlife observation.

Directions: Travel south on State Hwy. 17 out of Rhinelander; immediately after crossing the Pelican River, travel southeast along gated trail for 1/4 mi.; follow left fork to DNR microwave tower in Natural Area. Park and approach preserve on foot.
NOTE: Visitors are encouraged to check in at the Wisconsin Department of Natural Resources (DNR) Ranger Station (north of Hwy. 17) before entering preserve.

Kurtz Woods

The lush, deciduous canopy of trees ignites with autumnal splendor in the fall and a carpet of wildflowers blossoms abundantly in springtime.

bloodroot

Few remnants remain of the deep forests that characterized the pre-settlement era in southeastern Wisconsin. Kurtz Woods is one of them, all the more valuable because it is a relatively undisturbed southern mesic forest that hosts more than 82 species of trees and spring ephemerals. One of the plants once found here was ginseng (*Panex quinquefolium*), but heavy illegal collecting appears to have eliminated it from the preserve. Conservancy efforts may someday restore ginseng as a vital component of this natural area.

The forest is dominated by thick stands of sugar maple and American beech. White ash, basswood and black cherry constitute a shorter set of trees that spread east and west from the center of the preserve. The appearance of pole-size trees along the southeast boundary, evidence of logging in the 1930s, and an old granite quarry along the southwest edge, are the only reminders of earlier land use and the last signs of disturbance here.

A diverse assortment of spring wildflowers shares the forest floor with varying sizes of shrubs and young trees. These include hepatica, bloodroot, wild leek and the aptly named spring beauty. Kurtz Woods is designated as a State Natural Area because of this diversity and the quality of the intact forest.

The terrain of Kurtz Woods is the lightly rolling, sandy moraine of the Lake Michigan Coastal Zone. Kettle depressions and glacial boulders can be seen throughout the preserve. Cultivated fields and pastures surround Kurtz Woods, a property that was in the local Kurtz family since the 1800s. Brothers Earl and Clarence Kurtz donated the land to the Conservancy in 1980 and remain volunteer stewards of the property, along with a local ecologist.

Even before acquisition by the Conservancy, the preserve served as an outdoor laboratory for plant ecologists, naturalists and other UW scientists. It continues to be used as such and as a site for field trips by various groups.

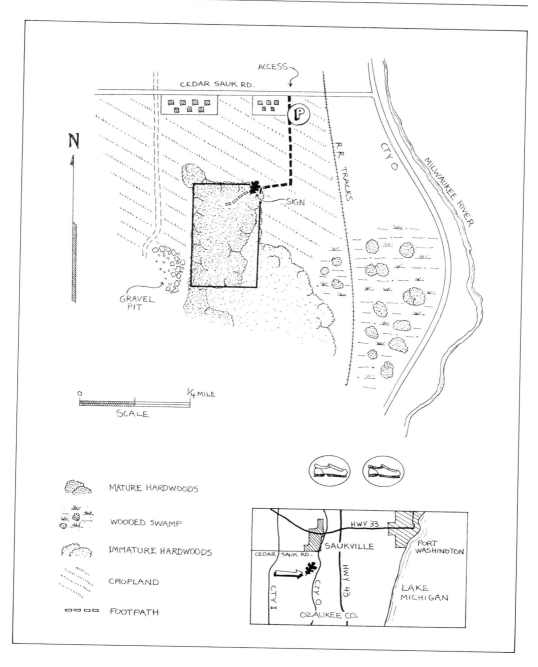

Protected: 31 Acres. Protection Goal: 31 Acres.
Southeastern Wisconsin. Located in Ozaukee County just south of Saukville in the Town of Grafton. Designated as a State Natural Area. Used extensively for education and research by the UW-Milwaukee and groups from the UW Cedar-Sauk Field Station nearby. Owned and managed by The Nature Conservancy of Wisconsin. Open to visitors for hiking and observation.

Directions: From intersection of Hwy. 33 & Cty. Hwy. O in Saukville, travel south on O approx. 1 mi. to intersection of Cedar Sauk Rd.; turn west (right) for less than 1 mi. to reach access road going south for 1/2 mi. to the northeast corner of the woods. Parking is allowed along this road.

Leopold
Memorial Woods

Tall trees and rocky out-croppings share a habitat and the name of a man who made conservation an honored legacy.

marsh marigolds

Aldo Leopold left such a deep and lasting impression on the lore of conservation in this country that any tract of land named for him holds a certain magic. The Leopold Memorial Woods is such a place. Part of the extensive Baraboo Hills region of southwestern Wisconsin, the Woods contain this area's characteristic sandstone ridges, a mix of oak and pine forest and an intermittent stream running diagonally through the preserve.

Dramatic outcroppings of conglomeritic rock are the dominant physical feature of the Woods. Sheer sandstone ridges from 40- to 50-feet high run along the northern section and incorporate a small cave and escarpment. Baraboo quartzite and sandstone characterize the area's geology, while rocky Baraboo silt loam is found in the southwest half.

Both southern and northern forest types thrive here. Tree species include red and white oak, red and sugar maple, yellow birch, white pine, basswood and a large hemlock relic. While dry-mesic forest dominates the forest community of the preserve, varieties of northern dry species also exist along the north- and south-facing ridges of the shaded-cliff communities.

Running water in this forest is provided by a stream that flows through a valley from one corner of the preserve to another. A smaller valley with a spring also flows to the north. The Leopold Memorial Woods provides an important water source for deer in the area. Birdlife attracted to this densely forested area includes the acadian flycatcher and waterthrush, both located in the hemlock/maple woods.

The biotic and historical assets of this area prompted naturalists from the UW-Madison's Kumlien Club, trustees of the Aldo Leopold Memorial Trust, to purchase the first 40 acres of the preserve in 1954. This was turned over to The Nature Conservancy in 1967. Additional land purchases followed, bringing the preserve to its present size.

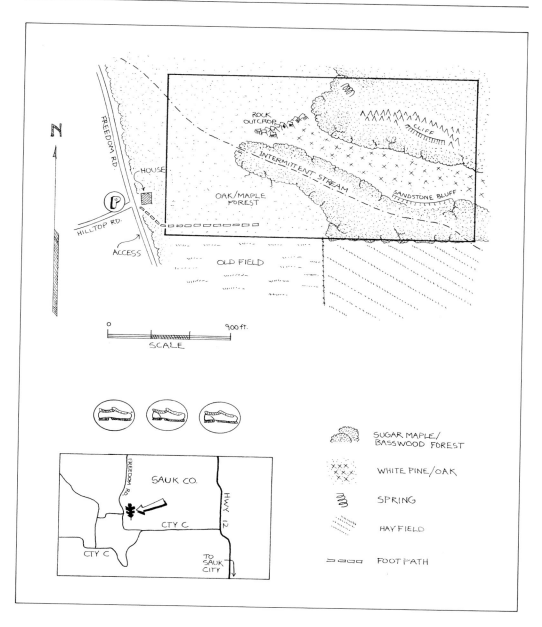

Protected: 83 Acres. Protection Goal: 100 Acres.
Southwestern Wisconsin.
Located in Sauk County on
the southern edge of the
Baraboo Hills region, north-
east of Sauk City. Owned and managed by
The Nature Conservancy of Wisconsin.
Open to visitors for hiking and observation.

Directions: Travel west on Cty. Hwy. C
(off US Hwy. 12 between Baraboo and Sauk
City) for 4 mi. to Freedom Rd.; travel 2 mi.
on Freedom Rd. to old log house on right
near intersection of Hilltop Rd. Park near
the Y-intersection and hike approx. 50-100
yds. on an old roadbed (past abandoned
shacks) to southwest corner of preserve.
A compass is advised since there are no
cleared paths.

Mink River Estuary

Nature's stake in this remarkable wetland is a strong one, an ancient pact between land and water to preserve an enchanting wilderness.

Lake Michigan shoreline

Mink River Estuary is a rare natural sanctuary — one of the few high-quality estuaries remaining in this country. It is a wetland ecosystem that supports dozens of wildlife and plant species. An estuary is an area created when river water mixes with water from large lakes or the ocean. As a spawning habitat and source of organic detritus, these productive estuaries are vital to the Lake Michigan ecosystem. But they are fragile. Most estuaries along the Great Lakes have been destroyed because they cannot easily share precious shoreline with human development.

The Mink River Estuary is considered the most "pristine" of its kind. It begins at the alkaline spring-fed headwaters of the Mink River and empties into nearby Rowley's Bay. It is an important spawning ground for fish and a critical migration site for birds. More than 200 bird species may pass through the area annually, including Cooper's hawk, a state-threatened species. Blue-winged teal, mallard, wood duck and black duck are present as nesting pairs, along with great blue herons, black terns, black-crowned night herons, herring gulls, bitterns, marsh hawks and common loons. In late summer and fall, double-breasted cormorants and red-breasted mergansers can be seen and there is evidence of habitation by the bald eagle and sandhill crane.

Wetlands' wildlife found at Mink River include beaver, porcupine, muskrat, raccoon and white-tailed deer. A variety of native snakes and frogs also inhabits the area.

The diverse vegetation in the estuary features communities from cedar trees to wild rice. Two state-threatened species are found here, the dune thistle (*Cirsium pitcheri*) and the dwarf lake iris (*Iris lacustris*). Lowland forest, dominated by white cedar, surrounds the edges of the emergent marsh.

The marsh itself is inhabited by willow, red-osier dogwood and alder. Sedges, blue joint grass and other emergent wetland species form the ground cover and continue through the wet meadow section. Sedge meadow and reed grass stands occur in the upstream shallow marsh portion of the wetland. Bulrush is the most ubiquitous species in the deep marsh area of the estuary. This and other deep marsh varieties serve to protect the inland communities by withstanding wave and seiche action from the lake. Many springs and intermittent streams saturate the forest floor as they feed into the river. Water lilies and water milfoil represent the submergent community of Mink River.

A history of the area reflects both Indian settlement and America's pioneer movement. Logging and farming cut a swath in the land over many generations, followed by a burgeoning tourism industry that is the peninsula's chief industry today. Yet one of the most dramatic influences on the quality of the estuary is the change in lake level. As the marsh goes from exposed sediment to deep water and back again, the mix of vegetation keeps any one natural community from being preeminent.

Despite development and use, changing fortunes and careful local conservation over time helped protect the freshwater estuary in much the same condition as when it was inhabited by the Potawotami Indians more than a century ago.

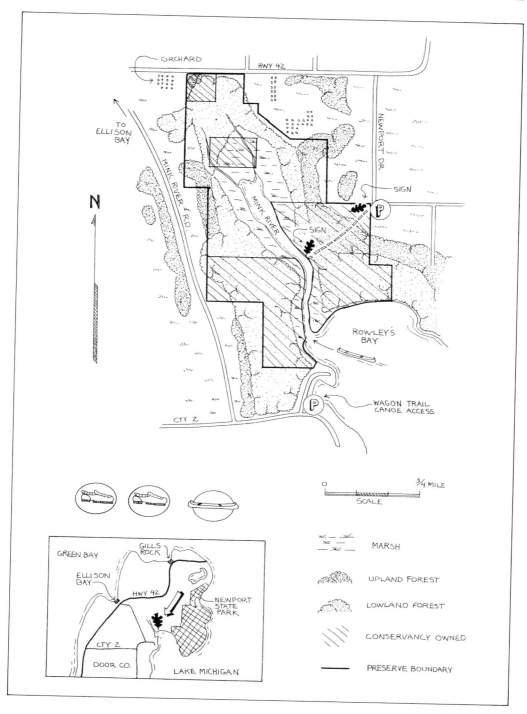

ORCHARD

HWY 42

TO ELLISON BAY

N

MINK RIVER RD.

MINK RIVER

NEWPORT DR.

SIGN

P

SIGN

ROWLEY'S BAY

WAGON TRAIL CANOE ACCESS

P

CTY Z

0   ¾ MILE

SCALE

MARSH

UPLAND FOREST

LOWLAND FOREST

CONSERVANCY OWNED

PRESERVE BOUNDARY

GREEN BAY

GILLS ROCK

ELLISON BAY

HWY 42

NEWPORT STATE PARK

CTY Z

DOOR CO.

LAKE MICHIGAN

**Protected: 769 Acres.
Protection Goal: 1500
Acres.** Northeastern
Wisconsin. Located in Door
County on the eastern shore
of the peninsula at Rowley's
Bay, southeast of the Village of Ellison Bay.
Considered one of the prime wetlands of its
type in the nation. Various unconnected
parcels of land make up the preserve.
Owned and managed by The Nature Con-
servancy of Wisconsin. Open to visitors for
observation on foot or by canoe.

Directions: From intersection of Hwy. 57
& Hwy. 42 in Sister Bay, travel 2 mi. north
on 42 to Cty. Z; turn east (right) on Z to
the Wagon Trail Campground on Rowley's
Bay. Boat landing and canoe rental are
available. Follow shoreline north to the
mouth of the Mink River.

Muehl Springs

creek in winter

Beneath a vista of steeply rolling forested hills, a clear-running stream meanders through wet natural meadow.

The undulating boundary line of Muehl Springs encircles an abundant southern sedge meadow that spreads east along the shore of the Sheboygan River. The most dominant element of this preserve is the high-quality spring that originates there and runs through the center of the tract alongside the rocky deposits of a glacial moraine. As many as 15 small springs feed into the stream from the marshy shallows nearby. More than 20 aquatic plants have been identified in this diverse stream, including watercress, duckweed, arrowhead and several species of manna grass.

As many as eight species of sedge grow undisturbed along the shore, in particular *Carex stricta* and *C. aquatilis*. The rich wetland community of Muehl Springs contains many herbs such as fleabane, goldenrod and the blue flag iris.

Shrub-carr spread across much of the land spanning north and south of the stream. Tamarack is found throughout the meadow area, along with swamp birch and meadow sweet.

A large grove of aspen can be seen on high ground just north of the highway bridge crossing the stream. The northeast upland portion of Muehl Springs, east of the highway, contains hardwood stands of beech and sugar maple trees. Among wildlife observed in and around Muehl Springs are white-tailed deer, wood duck and beaver.

Muehl Springs Preserve was presented to the Conservancy in 1986 by George and Herbert Roth as a memorial to their uncle, Philip Mathes, and their mother, Adele Mathes Roth.

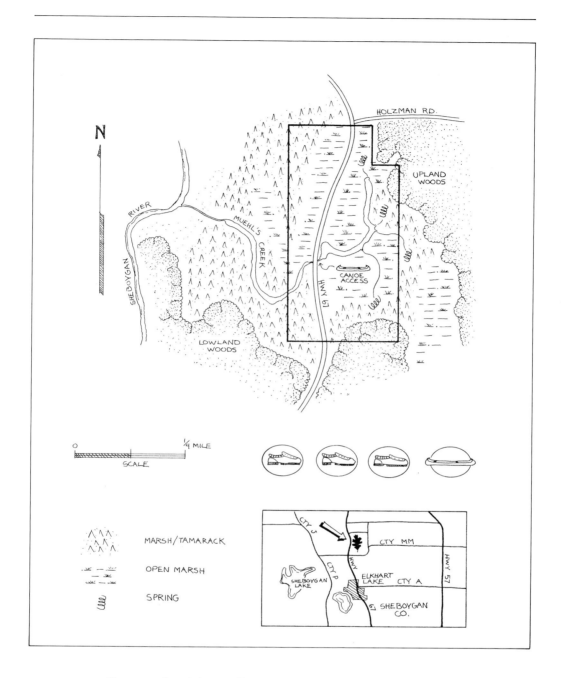

Protected: 75 Acres. Protection Goal: 210 Acres.
Southeastern Wisconsin. Located in Sheboygan County north of Elkhart Lake in Rhine Township. Owned and managed by The Nature Conservancy of Wisconsin. Open to visitors for nature walks and wildlife observation.

Directions: From Elkhart Lake, travel north on Hwy. 67 for approximately 2 mi.; the preserve, divided by the Hwy., lies east and west of the road.

Nelson Oak Woods

Venture into this woodland and experience the serenity of southern Wisconsin's precious rural landscape.

white oak.

Southern dry-mesic woods dominate the scene in this southeastern preserve. Nelson Oak Woods, as its name suggests, boasts a fine stand of oak trees along its upland section. Some of these, the white oaks in particular, fit the romantic description of a "wide oak" in their large, open-grown maturity. Red and black oak trees are also found here, in a forest that has made a strong comeback despite steady grazing before 1950. Lesser stands of shagbark hickory and black cherry are also present.

But Nelson Oak Woods is interesting for other reasons. A successional pattern of vegetation development is apparent throughout the preserve. The upland forest grades southwest to a small swamp forest and ephemeral ponds. The southern boundary runs along Scuppernong Creek, an area that supports small springs and high-quality vegetation. An unusual stand of yellow birch (*Betula alleghceniensis*) also thrives in the lowland, unusual because it is rarely found this far south. Other lowland species include the American elm, trembling aspen, sedges, cattails, wild sarsaparilla and hackberry.

A large variety of breeding birds is attracted to the woodland and swamp community mix at Nelson Oak Woods. The large, tall trees in the oak/cherry forest are home to the cerulean warbler and blue-grey gnatcatcher. Woodpecker populations and other hole-nesting birds are seen in the standing and fallen deadwood. Great-horned owls, red-tailed hawks and turkey vultures are recorded in the woods and along the wood's edge. In the wetter sites, the shrub and bramble habitat draws the mourning warbler, blue-winged warbler and other wetland denizens. Area residents report sightings of scarlet tanagers, ovenbirds, rufous-sided towhees and, near the ponds, wood ducks.

Donation of the land was made between 1972 and 1979 by Charles and Mary Nelson. Their objective in making the gift was to preserve the tract for education and research as well as provide a protected sanctuary for breeding birds. The Nelson's wishes are shared and honored by the Conservancy in the management of a rich preserve.

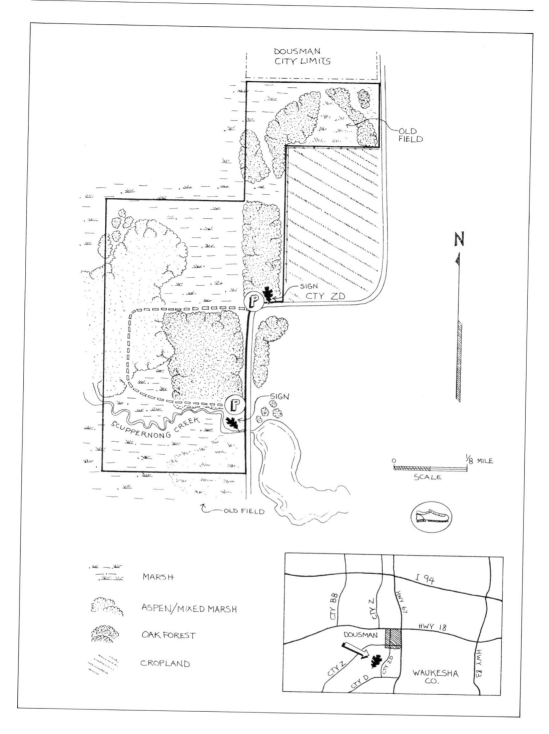

Protected: 115 Acres. Protection Goal: 115 Acres. Southeastern Wisconsin. Located in Waukesha County, south of Dousman. This southern forest habitat is widely used for education and research by classes from the UW-Waukesha Center campus and other study groups. Owned by The Nature Conservancy of Wisconsin. Managed in cooperation with UW-Waukesha Center. Open to visitors for hiking and observation.

Directions: Travel south on State Hwy. 67 off I-94 for 3 mi. to US Hwy. 18; travel west on 18 for 1/2 mi. then turn south on ZD (Main St.) in Dousman; follow Main St. through town to stop sign; continue south for approx. 3/4 mi. to sharp right (west) turn and go for 1/4 mi. until sharp left (south) turn. Park on outside of that curve and follow foot trail south through woods to creek.

Omro Prairie

Wild grasses have the right-of-way again in this strip of native Wisconsin prairie.

tall prairie grasses

In what must be one of the most unusual preserves owned by The Nature Conservancy of Wisconsin lies a remnant of protected prairie half a mile long and just 82-1/2 feet wide. Omro Prairie was once a railroad right-of-way. The land was abandoned by the Chicago/Milwaukee/St. Paul/Pacific Railroad and sold to the Conservancy in 1975. Old railroad ties and rails are gone and what remains is a valuable wet- to dry-mesic prairie community reminiscent of the state's pre-settlement days. Cultivated fields surround the site on two sides.

More than 62 species of prairie plants are identified in Omro Prairie, named for the town just one mile north of the site. Among species found here are slough grass, shooting star, closed gentian, common horsetail, a species of meadow rue and several shrubs, bur oak and dogwood.

The quality and variety of growth are the result of early fencing of the right-of-way and occasional burnings to prevent shrub growth. This prairie is near the northeastern limit of the range for this type of plant community in Wisconsin and, as such, has significant educational value.

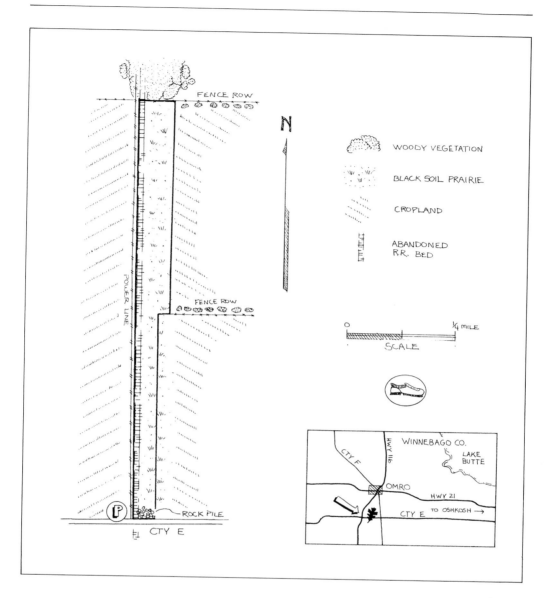

FENCE ROW

N

WOODY VEGETATION

BLACK SOIL PRAIRIE

CROPLAND

ABANDONED R.R. BED

POWER LINE

FENCE ROW

0   ¼ MILE

SCALE

WINNEBAGO CO.

CTY F
HWY 116
LAKE BUTTE
OMRO
HWY 21
CTY E
TO OSHKOSH →

ROCK PILE

CTY E

Protected: 5 Acres. Protection Goal: 7 Acres.
Eastern Wisconsin. Located in Winnebago County just south of the Town of Omro and west of Oshkosh. The narrow strip of land was once a railroad right-of-way. Owned by The Nature Conservancy and managed cooperatively with local volunteers. Used extensively for research and education purposes. Open to visitors for hiking and observation.

Directions: Travel west from Oshkosh on Cty. Hwy. E for approx. 9 mi. to the intersection with Cty. F (Job Road). Continue west on E for 1/4 mi. past the junction. Preserve lies north and adjacent to the highway. Park along the wide shoulder of the road.

Page Creek Marsh

Against a fall sky near still water, marsh plants form a protective cover over a habitat for a winged migration.

coots

Page Creek Marsh, named for the stream that runs nearby, is a high-quality wetland preserve with a stretch of upland grasses along the northern edge. This pairing of marsh meadow areas attracts a diverse population of water fowl and rare meadow birds. But at the heart of Page Creek Marsh is its value as a staging area for sandhill cranes during their fall migration. A secure, deep-water habitat — rich with emergent aquatic plants — provides cover for large numbers of birds every season.

The size and undisturbed quality of Page Creek Marsh lend further significance to its protection. The dominant community here is emergent aquatic, resplendent with an abundance of cattails, bladderwort, duckweed and arrow-head. Northern sedge meadow covers 30 percent of the land. Shrub-carr or open water account for another 25 percent. Various sedge species and bluejoint grass dominate the meadow section, crossed by a railroad right-of-way. Small willow and dogwood grow in the shrubby areas. South of the tracks, the sedge and cattail communities intermingle.

Gently rolling farmland borders the upland — a hint of the preserve's early history of grazing. Fortunately, previous use left no permanent mark on Page Creek Marsh, another of its attributes.

The first 69-acre section of Page Creek Marsh under Conservancy protection was a gift to the Wisconsin Chapter from Barbara Sheehan in 1986.

Protected: 69 Acres. Protection Goal: 445 Acres. Southcentral Wisconsin. Located in Marquette County south of Packwaukee Township. Owned and managed by The Nature Conservancy of Wisconsin. **Special Access only.** Contact the Conservancy office at 1045 E. Dayton St., Rm. 209, Madison, WI 53703 for more information or call (608) 251-8140.

Pan Hollow

maple leaves

Steep, shaded cliffs share a serene setting with tall forest trees and dewy woodland plants flowering among the rocks.

Pan Hollow is the local name given to the wooded valley where the Conservancy has protected two nearly adjacent parcels of land — the Bruckert Tract and the Gerald Scott Memorial Woods. This extensively wooded preserve contains a pleasing variety of geologic formations in a compact area.

The northwest section is characterized by the presence of Baraboo quartzite and relatively flat upland. Both oak and maple trees of a southern dry-mesic forest are found. This forest changes to southern mesic along the lower, eastern elevations. The terrain then slopes dramatically towards the eastern and southeastern portions of the preserve, dropping 120 feet in 400 feet. East of this cliff area the land forms an intermittent stream bottom containing hornbeam and Turk's-cap lily.

The lands of Pan Hollow were acquired by the Conservancy in 1970 to preserve their biological quality and protect an important educational opportunity. Funds for the project were raised by students of Gerald R. Scott, who taught biology at Baraboo High School for many years and remains active in a number of conservation organizations.

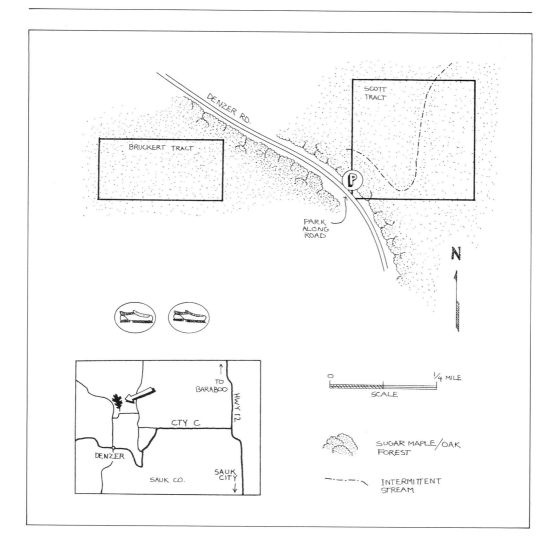

Protected: 65 Acres. Protection Goal: 300 Acres. Southwestern Wisconsin. Located in Sauk County in the Baraboo Hills region, just north of the Town of Denzer. Lies midway between two other Conservancy preserves, Pine Hollow and Leopold Memorial Woods. Owned and managed by The Nature Conservancy of Wisconsin. Used widely for educational purposes and open to visitors for hiking and observation.

Directions: Travel west on County Hwy. C (off US Hwy. 12 between Baraboo and Sauk City) for 7 mi. to Denzer; travel north on Denzer Rd. out of Denzer for 2-1/2 mi. to site on the east side of road.

Pickeral Lake Fen

Something rare inhabits the land here, as though tales of nature past and present were whispered in the thickness of the rushes.

Blanding's turtle

There *is* something special about Pickeral Lake Fen. This unspoiled community is among the rarest wetland types found in North America and one of the few under conservation protection. Several rare or endangered species are protected here, some in such abundance as to belie their endangered status. Because of its rich natural history, Pickeral Lake Fen is a dedicated State Natural Area.

The preserve is characterized by a high-quality calcareous, or calcium-based fen sloping from a glacial ridge and an oak opening along the western boundary. A sizable population of rare beaked spike-rush (*Eleocharis rostellata*) — considered the largest in the state — dominates the fen. Dozens of northern kittentails (*Besseya bullii*), a state-endangered species, are present along with pitcher plants (*Sarracenia purpurea*), seldom seen in "salt marsh" environments like this. Ciliated brome grass, Canada bluejoint grass, willows and other wetland species thrive in the surrounding marshland. A diverse emergent aquatic community is evident along the uneven shoreline of the 27-acre spring-fed Pickeral Lake that lies to the north just beyond the present preserve boundary.

The animals of Pickeral Lake Fen add to the unique nature of this preserve. The rare Blanding's turtle (*Emydoidea blandingi*) lives protected here and sandhill cranes are known to nest among the cattails along the lake's edge. In the lake itself, starhead topminnows, an uncommon fish on the state's endangered list, are seen in large numbers.

The pristine quality of Pickeral Lake Fen exists because the area is left largely undisturbed. Grazing and cutting on the adjacent lands have long since ceased, allowing valuable prairie habitat to reestablish along the northern oak-tree border. The Conservancy has owned and managed the land since it was donated in 1985 by Gerald and Signe Emmerich and Roy and Eleanor Muth. They made their gifts after first voluntarily registering their tracts with The Nature Conservancy. The preserve includes a conservation easement donated by the Emmerichs to serve as protection for the calcareous fen community.

Protected: 51 Acres. Protection Goal: 51 Acres. Southeastern Wisconsin. Located in Walworth County less than 2 mi. from the intersection of Pickeral Lake Rd. and Cty. J. Considered one of the rarest wetland types in North America and dedicated as a State Natural Area. Owned and managed by The Nature Conservancy of Wisconsin. **Special Access only.** Contact the Conservancy office at 1045 E. Dayton St., Rm. 209, Madison, WI 53703, for more information or call (608) 251-8140.

Pine Hollow

Undisturbed forest, sloping cliffs and deep valleys merge to create the breathtaking image of a natural gem set in the Baraboo Hills.

*white pines
first quarter moon*

Pine Hollow presents the visitor with one of the most interesting preserves found in this unique unglaciated area of Wisconsin. Here, a widely varying topography encourages much diverse vegetation, including woodland, stream, prairie opening and cliff communities. The mature northern hardwood forest at Pine Hollow supports a fine breeding bird community. At least three rare plant species are protected here — ginseng (*Panax quinquefolium*), sword moss (*Bryoxiphium norvegicum*) and a saxifrage (*Sullivantia renifolia*). The undisturbed quality of plant and animal communities at Pine Hollow, plus the rich geological history of the area, influenced its designation as a State Natural Area.

Forest trees cover a large percentage of the preserve. Along the steep ravine formed by the flow of an intermittent stream grow many sizes of hemlock trees and, on the upper edges of the sandstone cliffs, large white pines. Oak stands can be seen in the uplands on the eastern edge of the preserve and both maple and birch communities are found in the lower valley near the stream.

The majestic ravines that characterize this region occur at Pine Hollow. The site drops 280 feet over the distance of a half-mile and features cliff walls rising up to 80 feet. One huge bluff has an undercut ledge that may have been used as a rockshelter in prehistoric times.

Prairie and barrens plants grow in the sandy areas along the top of the west-facing bluff, including arrow-wood, huckleberry and blueberry.

Animal communities at Pine Hollow are equally influenced by the geography of this area. Birds such as the Canada warbler suggest the presence of northern species and the Louisiana waterthrush represents a species of southern Appalachian origin. The prairie community attracts species like the badger and there is evidence of deer as well as fox, skunk and raccoon.

Pine Hollow came into Conservancy possession during 1964 and 1965, largely through the efforts of Edith Seymour Jones in memory of her husband, Fred R. Jones, a noted plant pathologist at the UW-Madison. The south forty is named in his honor.

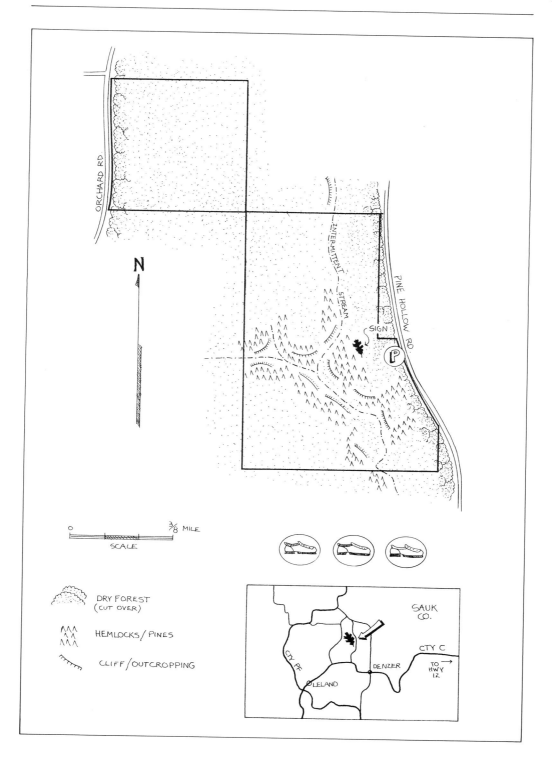

SCALE
0 ⅜ MILE

DRY FOREST
(CUT OVER)

HEMLOCKS / PINES

CLIFF / OUTCROPPING

Protected: 144 Acres. Protection Goal: 200 Acres. Southwestern Wisconsin. Located in Sauk County as part of the Baraboo Hills region, just northwest of the Town of Denzer. Designated a State Natural Area. Owned and managed by The Nature Conservancy of Wisconsin. Open to visitors for limited hiking and observation.

Directions: Travel west on County Hwy. C (off US Hwy. 12 between Baraboo and Sauk City) through Denzer approx. 1-1/2 mi. to Pine Hollow Rd.; travel north on Pine Hollow Rd. for 1-1/2 mi. to top of hill. Property is marked by green and yellow signs on left side of road.

Sacia Memorial Ridge

driftless upland hills

Undulating prairieland and a stately old forest settle together like a hidden valley in the coulee country landscape.

The oak forest and dry prairie of Sacia Memorial Ridge have changed little from the terrain described in the original survey of 1848. There were white, black and bur oak then, as well as birch, aspen and a host of prairie species forming the undergrowth. The ratio of species may have changed and the forest expanded, but the relative isolation of this land has long helped to keep a high-quality Mississippi River bluff community virtually intact for generations.

Sacia Memorial Ridge stands in the driftless, or unglaciated, area of southwestern Wisconsin where sloping ridges and rolling lowlands are punctuated by furrows of deep alluvium, or river sediment. A portion of the long ridge running through the preserve peaks in two knolls that rise 60 and 100 feet, respectively. These knolls offer a spectacular view of the Mississippi River valley to the west. Forest covers most of the site, dominated by oak hickory species on the south side of the ridge and mesic forest — popple and white birch — on the north.

A small prairie remnant grows along the south slope of the higher knoll, settled with prairie species like black-eyed Susan and spiderwort as well as an understory of blackberries. Trillium and interrupted fern are found along the northern slopes. Other plants add color and interest at Sacia, including yarrow, wood anemone, jack-in-the-pulpit, shooting star, evening primrose,

red baneberry and pasque flower. Visitors are cautioned that poison ivy also grows in abundance throughout the preserve.

Wildlife finds sanctuary in the woods of Sacia. White-tailed deer, raccoons and cottontail rabbits freely reside. Woodcock, ruffed grouse, rose-breasted grosbeak, towhee, catbird, field sparrow, pewee and flicker have all been spotted here, too.

Sacia Memorial Ridge is named in memory of a local family who continue to operate the adjacent apple orchard. One parcel was purchased by friends at the University of Wisconsin-Madison to honor Niles Sacia, who had a great interest in conserving Wisconsin's natural landscape. A second parcel honors Fred and Lily Sacia, pioneer apple growers of western Wisconsin. The preserve was donated to the Conservancy in 1975 and, according to the wishes of the Sacia family, is available for educational purposes.

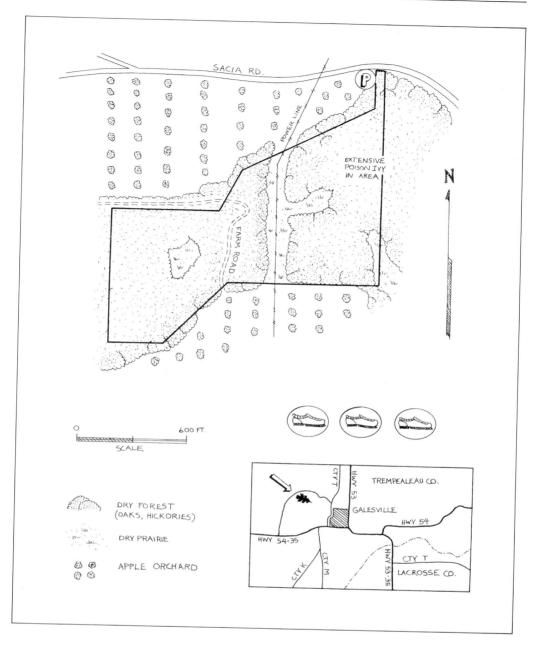

Protected: 29 Acres. Protection Goal: 29 Acres. Westcentral Wisconsin. Located in Trempealeau County northwest of Galesville. The preserve is faced on two sides by the Sacia Apple Orchards. Owned and managed by The Nature Conservancy of Wisconsin. Used for educational purposes. Open to visitors for limited hiking and observation.

Directions: From the intersection of US Hwy. 53 and Hwy. 35 in Galesville, travel 1 mi. west of Hwy. 54-35 to Cty. T; travel north on T almost 2 mi. to Sacia Rd. and turn left (west); follow Sacia Rd. to point where power line intersects road.

Preserve lies south of road and a stretch of orchard. Visitors should use the farm roads crossing the preserve as trails to avoid poison ivy patches. Most of the area can be seen from these roads.

Schluckebier Sand Prairie

The prairie has been recovered here as if to signal the timeless and boundless strength of nature.

shooting stars

When white settlers first came to Wisconsin's Sauk Prairie area in the 1840s, prairie covered over 20,000 acres of the landscape that spread before them. Those early images of tall grass and blooming paint drops of color stretching beyond the horizon are smaller now and merge into a scene of woods and farmland. Schluckebier Sand Prairie is an important remnant of dry prairie containing more than 158 species of prairie plants. Over half a century ago, it too was under the plow. But the sandy soil did not respond well to cultivation and it was soon left to self-restoration. The land became prairie once again.

Schluckebier (pronounced SHLUCK′-e-beer) Sand Prairie lies close to the glacial boundary of the driftless, or unglaciated, area of Wisconsin. The fact that it is a naturally restored community makes this preserve of special interest to the Conservancy. The rare bush clover (*Lespedeza leptostachya*) grows here, a prairie plant not seen in Wisconsin for some 90 years until 1969, when it was discovered in three localities, including Schluckebier.

The eight-acre northern section of the preserve is a significant *tallgrass prairie* that effectively recreates — though on a small scale — the majesty of this prairie community. Statuesque species such as big bluestem (*Andropogon Gerardi*) and Indian grass (*Nutans avenaceum*) dominate the landscape of prairie vegetation. A variety of sedges and asters are found in both sites, along with blazing star, evening primrose, catchfly, goat's beard, red sorrel and other native plants.

Careful management over the years has lessened the encroachment of trees such as black locust, cherry and aspen found along the preserve boundaries. Nonetheless, the bordering woods encourage a healthy bird population here. Mourning doves, indigo bunting, dickcissel, bobolink and cedar waxwing have been sighted.

The Conservancy acquired the Schluckebier preserve in two transactions, as a gift and through a trade. In 1969, area native Donald Kindschi purchased a 20-acre parcel in the southern site from the Schluckebier family, who had owned it for 100 years. He then donated the land to the Conservancy. In 1976, a neighboring farmer traded the northern sand barrens tract and an easement through the locust woods for a seven-acre section of still-farmable land in the southeast corner of the original section. Schluckebier Sand Prairie — two tracts separated by a road and 200 yards of farm and forest — represents the most secure prairie remnant within miles. Careful management encourages the spread of native prairie species on the property. The diversity and history of this preserve have already made it an important source of seed for prairie community restoration at other area sites.

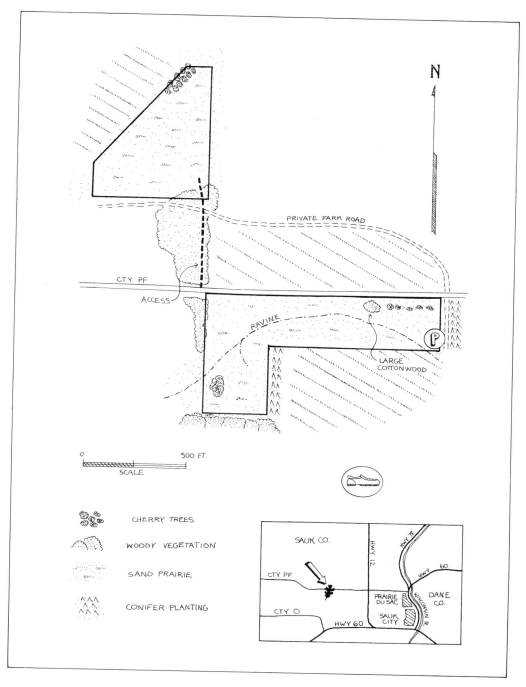

Protected: 23 Acres. Protection Goal: 30 Acres. Southwestern Wisconsin. Located in Sauk County west of Prairie du Sac. The preserve is divided into two tracts of natural prairie situated on either side of a county road. Owned and managed by The Nature Conservancy of Wisconsin. Open to visitors for nature observation and bird watching.

Directions: From the intersection of US Hwy. 12 and Cty. PF near Prairie du Sac, travel west on PF for 1-1/2 mi. The preserve stands in two sections. One section lies south of the road (14+ acres) and another (8+ acres) section is located north of the road; follow footpath approx. 200 yds. through a black locust woods to the hilltop. Park just off the farm road on the east side of the larger section.

Snapper
Memorial Prairie

Like a western flatland, the small prairie lies low against the sky with subtle accents of textured color in the flowering grasses.

grasshopper

Snapper Memorial Prairie is a precious remnant of what was once a 2,500-acre low prairie in the Crawfish River floodplain. It remains a virgin prairie, never plowed as the land around it was. Instead, the owners mowed it for hay and did a burning in the fall, treatment that helped preserve many prairie plant species, including at least three threatened or endangered ones. Indian plantain (*Cacalia tuberosa*), from the state list of threatened species, grows here along with white lady-slipper (*Cypripedium candidum*) and prairie milkweed (*Asclepias sullivanti*), from the endangered list.

A rich collection of low prairie plants represents the more common species that populate Snapper Prairie. Big bluestem, little bluestem, prairie dock and northern dropseed also grow here. Many showy prairie forbs, like the blazing star, coneflower and compass plant, add color to the site. The clay soil of the lowland prairie means moisture conditions can dramatically change the look of this preserve from dry to flooded, depending on rainfall.

Snapper Memorial Prairie is also home to indigenous birds and animals. Upland sandpipers nest on the prairie and populations of bobolinks and savanna sparrows are recorded. Opossum, rabbit, fox, mink, raccoon and white-tailed deer are found to roam this protected area between fields of soybeans and corn.

Since the area was settled in the 1870s, up to the time of sale to the Conservancy in 1978, the land that is Snapper Memorial Prairie had been owned by one family, the Millers. Funds for the purchase were donated by the children of a Milwaukee couple as a memorial to their parents, Arthur and Albena Snapper.

Preserved: 28.33 Acres. Preservation Goal: 29 Acres. Southeastern Wisconsin. Located in Jefferson County north of Lake Mills. Owned and managed by The Nature Conservancy of Wisconsin. **Special Access only.** For more information, contact the Conservancy office at 1045 E. Dayton, Rm. 209, Madison, WI 53703 or call (608) 251-8140.

South Bluff Oak Forest

Enter a forest world where woodland plants and animals thrive sheltered by a deep canopy of majestic trees.

lady-slipper orchids

South Bluff Oak Forest belongs to the Baraboo Hills region of southwestern Wisconsin, which makes it part of the largest intact block of woods in southern Wisconsin. This preserve is a picture of deep woods, meadowland and the sloping rock ridges that characterize the driftless, or unglaciated, areas of the state. As its name suggests, the South Bluff forest is dominated by oaks: white oak in a dry section to the east and red oak in the western mesic section. Species of pine, butternut, hickory, maple and ash are also found in the dry forest — basswood, cherry, aspen and ironwood in the mesic forest. After a history of logging, South Bluff Oak Forest has gone undisturbed for more than 80 years and the largest trees now stand mature.

There are few openings in the South Bluff forest, but two prairie-meadow areas exist, one of which provides habitat for the tubercled orchid (*Habenaria flava*), a plant that once appeared on the state threatened species list. A rare species of bush clover (*Lespedeza virginica*) grows in the southwest portion of South Bluff where the moist and shady conditions of the forest floor also support woodland ferns, ginseng and the spotted coral-root orchid. A 15-foot-high escarpment crosses the northwest corner of the preserve where drier conditions encourage some gooseberry and blueberry plants.

Two threatened species of wildlife — Cooper's hawk and the pickerel frog — are protected at South Bluff. Streams and springs occur here, fed by the Messenger Creek Gorge that runs from the southwest corner of Devil's Lake State Park. It is the site of an interior forest bird community of some significance. Breeding birds recorded here include the broad-winged hawk, redstart, and hooded, mourning and chestnut-sided warblers. Owls, chickadees, the white-breasted nuthatch, ovenbird and ruffed grouse are also found. Forest-habitat animals at South Bluff include white-tailed deer, raccoon and chipmunk.

Acquisition of South Bluff Oak Forest began in 1972 when the Conservancy received a gift of land from area resident and Conservancy member Donald Kindschi. A tract of South Bluff is named the Edith Kindschi Forest Preserve in honor of his mother. Adjacent parcels were acquired with Dr. Kindschi's help and named Steidtmann Forest Preserve and Roick Forest Preserve for families who had owned the land over several generations.

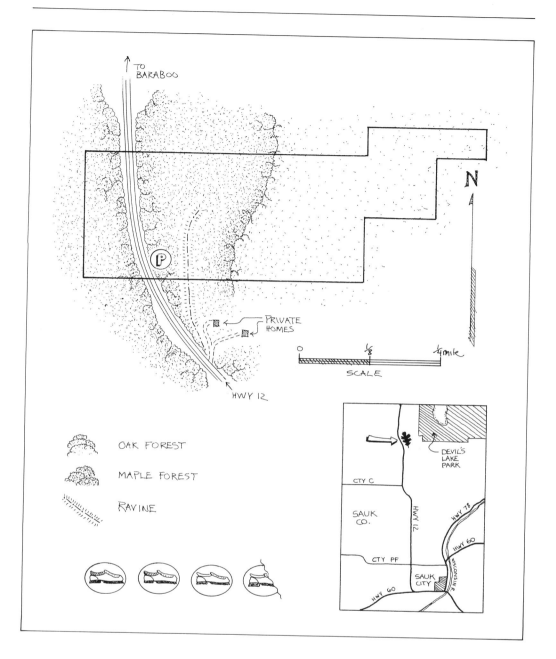

TO BARABOO

N

PRIVATE HOMES

HWY 12

0   ⅛   ¼ mile

SCALE

OAK FOREST

MAPLE FOREST

RAVINE

CTY C

SAUK CO.

DEVIL'S LAKE PARK

HWY 12

HWY 78

HWY 60

CTY PF

SAUK CITY

WISCONSIN R.

HWY 60

**Protected: 100 Acres.
Protection Goal: 100
Acres.** Southwestern
Wisconsin. Located in Sauk
County 1 mile south of
Devil's Lake between
Baraboo and Sauk City. Once known as
Sumpter Bluff, this preserve is part of the
overall Baraboo Hills project administered
by the Conservancy. Owned and managed
by The Nature Conservancy of Wisconsin.
Open to visitors for hiking and observation.

Directions: Travel north on US Hwy. 12
from Sauk City for 10 mi. past Badger
Ordnance site. The preserve lies east (right)
of the highway. Park along the shoulder of
the old roadway.

Spring Green Preserve

Nature's stillness echoes along the bluffs and dunes of this prairie desert, a stretch of river valley rich in diversity.

prickley pear cactus

It is known as the "Wisconsin Desert," this place where forest meets bluff and bluff levels off into flat, dry prairie. The Spring Green Preserve is one of the region's finest examples of dry prairie mixed with southern mesic forest and steep limestone cliffs. Situated on an ancient terrace of the Wisconsin River, now three miles to the south, the preserve unfolds in the driftless, or unglaciated, area of the state. Spring Green Preserve recalls the desert land of the American West, a land of cactus and lizards, sand dunes and dry grasses. Here, rich deposits of sand and limy cliffs left in the glacier's wake intermingle to support an ecosystem of immense value.

The diversity of plant and animal species and their unique interdependence on one another are of primary importance at Spring Green Preserve. An example of the essential link between species begins with the desert-like plant found here, the prickly pear cactus (*Opuntia compressa*). Its fleshy pads are food to the endangered ornate box turtle (*Terrapene ornata*) — Wisconsin's only terrestrial turtle — and the uncommon pocket gopher, whose tunnels provide cover for the bull snake and other reptile species at Spring Green Preserve. The gophers and other wildlife also forage at the roots of many plants here, helping to reduce the spread of grasses that discourage the growth of valuable prairie annuals and perennials.

Eleven species of reptiles are recorded at Spring Green Preserve, including three of Wisconsin's four species of lizards, the six-lined racerunner, five-lined skink and glass lizard, and the ornate box turtle. Though the six-lined racerunner and box turtle are each found in two or three other locations around the state, this is the only place they are known to co-exist. Along the eastern edge of the preserve, remnants of enclosures from an abandoned turkey farm serve as shelter for lizards, snakes, voles and other animals. Uncommon bird species such as vesper sparrow and lark sparrow also nest in the area.

Among the most unusual populations here are the invertebrates. Some are insects found nowhere else in Wisconsin: a constantly buzzing cicada (*Diceroprocta vitripennis*), one of five cicadas at Spring Green Preserve; the subtropical *Megacephala virginica*, one of eight tiger beetles recorded, and a predatory wasp. Spiders, such as the black widow and North America's largest wolf spider, also thrive in the preserve, and are part of an active nightlife among the rock ridges and sand dunes. The ecological chain is complete with a wide range of mammals, large and small.

Natural communities at Spring Green Preserve vary from a thick oak forest on the north side of a dry-lime prairie summit to wind-carved blowouts and sand barrens on the south-facing lower slopes. Cultivated land surrounds the preserve on several sides, along with mature pine groves planted as windbreaks.

Since the Conservancy acquired the Spring Green Preserve in 1971, management of the site has been as diverse as the habitats within. The Conservancy now works with the Wisconsin Natural Areas Preservation Council, local landowners and scientists from the University of Wisconsin to protect a unique community of plants and animals. This includes ongoing efforts to restore and maintain the sand prairie/oak barrens ecosystem of the Spring Green Preserve, frequently used for education and research.

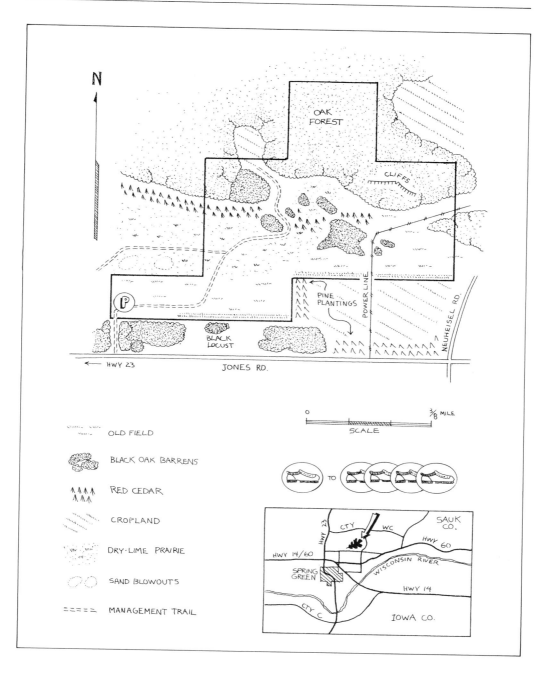

N

OLD FIELD

BLACK OAK BARRENS

RED CEDAR

CROPLAND

DRY-LIME PRAIRIE

SAND BLOWOUTS

MANAGEMENT TRAIL

OAK FOREST

CLIFFS

POWER LINE

PINE PLANTINGS

BLACK LOCUST

NEUHEISEL RD.

← HWY 23   JONES RD.

0   3/8 MILE
        SCALE

TO

SAUK CO.
CTY WC
HWY 23
HWY 60
HWY 14/60
WISCONSIN RIVER
SPRING GREEN
HWY 14
CTY C
IOWA CO.

Protected: 260 Acres. Protection Goal: 855 Acres. Southwestern Wisconsin. Located in Sauk County just north of Spring Green in the Wisconsin River valley. Begun as part of a 480-acre joint management agreement between The Nature Conservancy of Wisconsin, the private Head Foundation, the Wisconsin Natural Areas Preservation Council and local landowners. A 140-acre section of the Conservancy tract is a Designated State Natural Area. Used extensively for research and reseeding of other prairie-type preserves. Open to visitors for hiking and observation.

Directions: From the intersection of US Hwy. 14 and State Hwy. 23 near Spring Green, travel north on 23 for 1/2 mi. to intersection with Jones Rd. on the right (east); travel east on Jones Rd. for 3/4 mi. to preserve on the left of road. Turn in a dirt access road just past driveway leading to house trailer.

Summerton Bog

Stillness rules this marsh, where only the rustle of meadow grasses and the flutter of nesting birds stir the air.

tiger swallowtails

Summerton Bog is one of just a few remaining wetland areas of its kind in Wisconsin, a richly diverse system of animal and plant communities that exists in oscillating harmony. This diversity is especially unique because the "southern zone" Summerton Bog contains plant varieties — sedges, in particular — that are northern in type. This small, protected area also contains a wide variety of orchids and wildflowers along a western section of calcareous fen. Rising above the willowy grasses is a five-acre oak island that stands in marked contrast to the low vegetation all around.

Summerton Bog is part of a larger area known as the Endeavor Marsh, part of the Fox River watershed, and stands in a glacial lakebed where muck and peat soils support the various forest types and emergent aquatic communities. Water is at or near the surface year-round in the lowland areas, supplied by inflow from direct precipitation and five large artesian springs. The earliest maps of the area, dating back to the 1830s, show sedge meadow as the predominant vegetation. Subsequent land use for grazing, haying, logging and ditching disturbed the ecosystem and the meadows succumbed to an invasion of hydric shrubs or were lost altogether outside the preserve. Due to water-level fluctuations common to the wetland community, much of the meadow land was restored and no longer farmed. Many uncommon species of sedge and meadow flowers now grow throughout the site.

Among plant species found in the Summerton meadow are tussock sedge, sawgrass sedge, Canada bluejoint grass, aster species, Joe-pye-weed and goldenrod. Red-osier dogwood, bog birch and willows dominate the meadow, showing signs of a too-rapid invasion. Flowers in the fen include fringed gentians, yellow avens, bunchberry, yellow stargrass, yellow loosestrife, lobelia and as many as nine orchid species. These last include rein orchid, yellow lady-slipper, the threatened small white lady-slipper (*Cypripedim candidum*) and showy white lady-slipper.

Wildlife also finds refuge at Summerton Bog. The low, lush meadow and fen vegetation surrounded by tamaracks is a gathering place for nesting birds. As many as 65 species have been spotted. The Nashville warbler, veery, green heron and the song sparrow are just a few of the birds that reside in season. The bog is also an important nesting area for sandhill cranes.

The pickerel frog, once considered a threatened species in Wisconsin, is seen at Summerton Bog. White-tailed deer graze in abundance on the site and cause damage to the orchids by excessive browsing. The springs that dot the wetlands provide habitat for otters and an array of small aquatic organisms. Prescribed burning, ditch closure and native plant reseeding have been used to encourage the proliferation of sedge meadow vegetation and beautiful orchids.

The Conservancy began acquiring land for Summerton Bog in 1966 and purchased an additional parcel of 60 acres from landowners Lyman and Jane Stuart in 1977. The preserve is designated a National Natural Landmark and State Natural Area and serves as a key state resource for scientists studying the lifeforms and cycles of wetland ecosystems.

Protected: 428 Acres. Protection Goal: 600 Acres. Southcentral Wisconsin. Located in Marquette County approximately 3 mi. north of Portage. The wetland preserve is dedicated as a National Natural Landmark and is available for education and research. **Special Access only.** Owned and managed by The Nature Conservancy of Wisconsin. Contact the Conservancy office at 1045 E. Dayton St., Rm. 209, Madison, WI 53703, for more information or call (608) 251-8140.

Thousand's Rock Point Prairies

upland sandpiper

Small, rocky islands of prairie seem to float amidst the rich Wisconsin farmland, disturbed by nothing more than the season's change.

The dry limestone prairie remnants that make up Thousand's Rock Point Prairies enjoy several distinctions. For one, the tiny dual preserves stand in two counties separated by less than a mile of cultivated field. Most significantly, the original three acres of this preserve were the first land donation ever made to the Wisconsin Chapter of the Conservancy. The gift was made in 1964 by Stacy and Mildred Collins in honor of their father, Christian W. Thousand, who farmed the nearby land for many years. His deep appreciation of the prairie flowers that grew here was a feeling passed on to his children and honored in the legacy of this preserve.

A diverse natural community thrives in splendid isolation on these prairies, including 68 species of plants and more than 25 species of nesting birds. The thin and rocky soil makes the land unsuitable for cultivation though it is surrounded by farmed fields on all sides. Among the plants native to this patch of natural history are the pomme de prairie (*Psoralea esculenta*) and the green milkweed (*Asclepias viridiflora*), both species now uncommon in this region. A compact population of grasses and wildflowers grows here, including little and big bluestem grass, Solomon's seal, yellow Indian paintbrush, bird's-foot violet, wood betony, skullcap, the lovely pasque flower and valerian, seldom found in this habitat.

Thousand's Rock Point Prairies also provide nesting habitat for many birds, including six species of open-country sparrows — the grasshopper, vesper, Henslow's, savannah, song and field sparrows. In addition, the bobolink, upland sandpiper, eastern kingbird and dickcissel are often observed on the two sites.

The initial Dane County tract, donated by the Collins', was augmented in 1979 by Conservancy acquisition of an additional five acres in nearby Iowa County. The diversity and size of this prairie preserve make it a valuable lab for students of Wisconsin's early prairie environment.

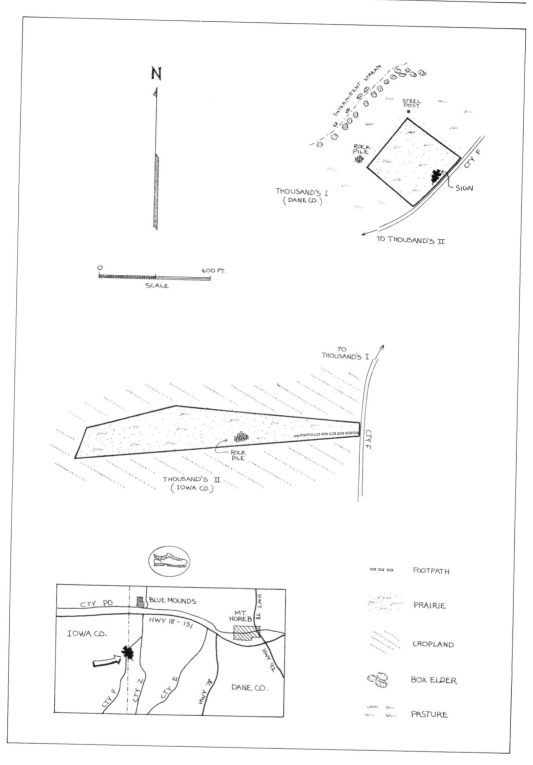

Protected: 8 Acres. Protection Goal: 36 Acres. Southwestern Wisconsin. Located in both Iowa and Dane Counties southwest of Blue Mounds. Made up of two land parcels separated by less than a mile. Owned and managed by The Nature Conservancy of Wisconsin. Open to visitors for nature study and bird watching.

Directions: Travel on US Hwy. 18/151 west from Mt. Horeb to the intersection with Cty. Hwy. Z on the southeastern edge of Blue Mounds; turn south on Z for 1-1½ mi. to intersection of Cty. Hwy. F. Travel 1 mi. on F to edge of the Dane County tract; second tract lies less than 1 mi. southwest from first in Iowa County.

Waubesa Wetlands

A vision of low marsh grass greets the eye for several miles along a nearly unbroken horizon of natural wetlands.

oxbow stream

Waubesa Wetlands is part of one of the most studied and valued water habitats in Wisconsin, covering more than 700 total acres. Past studies have investigated the geology of the land, the diversity of the plant and animal life, the biological productivity of the site and many other aspects of what is a remarkably undisturbed wetland. The Nature Conservancy tracts, in particular, contain several state-threatened species and uncommon community types.

Long termed a "living museum" of Wisconsin's native plant and animal communities, the Waubesa Wetlands is thought by ecologists to have once been a bay of now nearby Lake Waubesa. In its present incarnation, the wetlands exhibit a renowned natural diversity of springs, sedge meadows, floating mats and fen. The water source here is not the Lake — despite its proximity — but numerous small springs that erupt near the upland edge of the wetlands to provide a continuous flow of clear, cool water. One of the most impressive is Bogholt Deep Spring, part of a 40-acre tract donated by Carl and Julia Bogholt. The spring originates 12 feet beneath Deep Spring Creek from a cave lined with filamentous algae and purple-colored sulfur bacteria.

Southern sedge meadows, a state-threatened community, are found here. The meadows feature bluejoint grass and tussock sedge amid a scattering of sawgrass sedge, cattails and burr reed. A fen community of brome grass, aster, goldenrod and sage willow thrives in the cold limy spring water of the wetlands. Red osier dogwood, pussy willow and bog birch are part of a shrub carr community located along the western edge of the Conservancy tract. State-threatened or uncommon plants found and studied at Waubesa include the narrow-leaved fringed gentian (*Gentiana procera*), small water parsnip (*Berula pusilla*) and the yellow monkey flower (*Mimulus glabratus*).

Though human visitors find it difficult to traverse the marshy terrain, it is a welcome habitat for many species of waterfowl and other migrating birds. Waubesa is an important nesting stop for sandhill crane, the great blue heron, the American bittern, Canada goose and American coot as well as the blue-gray gnatcatcher, common yellowthroat and common grackle. Along the creek beds, a thriving population of Blanding's turtles (*Emydoidea blandingi*), another state-threatened species, is found. The waters of the Waubesa Wetlands preserve also provide a major fish spawning area, especially for northern pike in the early to mid-spring.

The Conservancy has acquired land for the Waubesa Wetlands preserve in the form of gifts and purchases since 1974. The sustained high quality of this preserve is due in large part to the support of many area residents and landowners who recognize the value of preserving such an important habitat.

The Conservancy continues to work closely in a conservation partnership with the Town of Dunn, Dane County, the Wisconsin Department of Natural Resources (DNR) and the Southern Wisconsin Wetlands Association in protecting the integrity of these noteworthy Waubesa Wetlands.

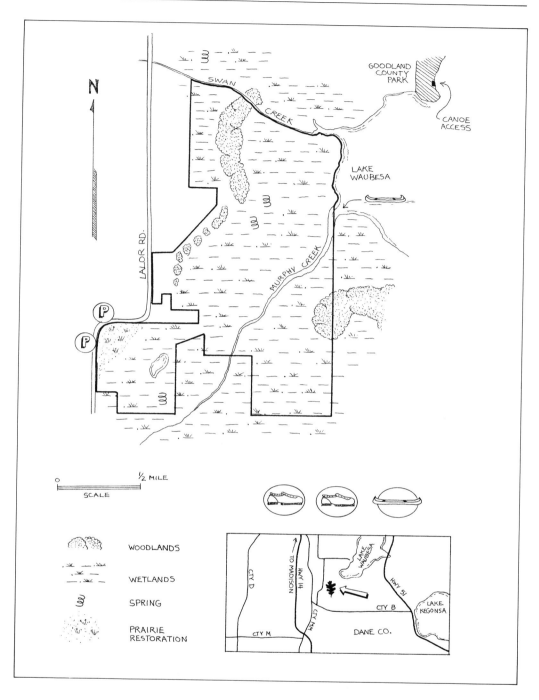

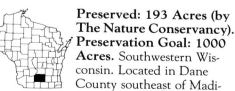

Preserved: 193 Acres (by The Nature Conservancy). Preservation Goal: 1000 Acres. Southwestern Wisconsin. Located in Dane County southeast of Madison at the southwest corner of Lake Waubesa. This preserve is part of a sizable wetland area widely used for scientific research and study. Owned and managed by The Nature Conservancy of Wisconsin. A neighboring preserve is owned and managed by the Wisconsin Department of Natural Resources. Open to visitors for limited hiking and observation.

Directions: From Madison, travel south on US Hwy. 14 to the intersection with Cty. MM; travel north on MM to Cty. B; turn right (east) on B for 1/4 mi. to Lalor Rd.; travel left (north) on Lalor for approx. 1-1/2 mi. to opening of preserve on the right.

Walter & Rose Zinn Preserve

red-breasted nuthatch

Abundant quiet fills this place where scenic lakes lie peacefully surrounded by a diversity of forest and swamp.

Just 35 miles from downtown Milwaukee, the Walter & Rose Zinn Preserve thrives undisturbed and unique. Acquired by the Conservancy as a gift from Rose Zinn in 1982, the site is characterized by a rare combination of two community types — pristine lake and tamarack swamp. The lakes on the preserve are encircled by some 70 acres of swamp and wet mesic forest species like white cedar, black spruce, balsam fir and jack pine. Mosses and other swamp groundcover, such as creeping snowberry and false solomon's seal, are also found along the shoreline. Beck Lake provides safe harbor for nesting and migrating waterfowl. Wood ducks, blue-wing teal and mallard are recorded in residence. In complementary contrast, Walters Lake to the north supports a large and pristine fish population, including northern pike and largemouth bass.

Rare plants found on the Zinn preserve include the small yellow lady-slipper (*Cypripedium parviflorum*), showy lady-slipper (*Cypripedium reginae*) and the slender bog arrow grass (*Triglochin palustris*). In keeping with a theme of natural diversity, the preserve contains sedge bog, southern mesic forest, swamp hardwood forest and shrub carr communities. Thus the site presents a fine mix of prairie grasses, dogwoods and willows, goldenrod and milkweed, sweet cicely and wild leek. A canopy of sugar maple trees draws a sizable population of forest breeding birds to the Zinn Preserve, such as the cedar waxwing, wood thrush and blackcapped chickadee. The land along the lakes remains in an original undisturbed state, making it an ideal site for research by University of Wisconsin and other scientists.

Protected: 121 Acres. Protection Goal: 875 Acres. Southeastern Wisconsin. Located in Washington County near Hartford in the Town of Erin. Owned and managed by The Nature Conservancy of Wisconsin. **Special Access only.** Widely used for research and study by University scientists and students. Contact the Conservancy office at 1045 E. Dayton St., Rm. 209, Madison, WI 53703 for more information or call (608) 251-8140.

Other Places We Save

Canada geese

The Nature Conservancy of Wisconsin maintains close ties with many government agencies, private organizations and individuals. The Conservancy often joins forces with conservation partners to secure protection of threatened natural lands. Such cooperation is necessary because scant financial resources for conservation would be severely taxed by individual efforts alone. We could not save the natural heritage of Wisconsin without it.

Thus, we share a deep concern for the safe-keeping of the biological and ecological history of Wisconsin and work together to save what we can. In some cases, the Conservancy makes an acquisition from available funds and, when payment is complete, transfers ownership to an appropriate steward such as the University or various local, state and national government agencies. The Conservancy frequently works alongside the Wisconsin Department of Natural Resources and other groups to help preserve large and valuable areas. While the Conservancy does not own or directly manage these preserves, we include them in this Directory because we're proud of the part we played in saving them.

Abraham's Woods

Spring finds this place most alive with a forest carpet of ephemeral wildflowers beneath the stark majesty of oak and maples.

trillium

Abraham's Woods was the first acquisition made by The Nature Conservancy in Wisconsin. This tract of deep woods grading into dry prairie was purchased by the Conservancy in 1961 and transferred to the University of Wisconsin–Madison soon after. Though the woods had been used as a woodlot over the past 100 years, cutting done on a selective basis helped preserve the overstory of trees and understory of herbs. The site was named for one previous owner, Ben Abraham, who collected maple sap here until his death.

This preserve is a valuable remnant of a climax, or terminal, forest and dry prairie combination. It represents the landscape of pre- and early-settlement Wisconsin, a magnificent and complex woods surrounded by wide expanses of prairie. Large red oaks are sparse but suggest the towering trees that prevailed at one time. Sugar maple and slippery elm now dominate the forest canopy. Basswood, yellowbud hickory, hackberry, black walnut and butternut are present in smaller numbers.

Preservation of this land has much to do with its topography. Along the western edge of the woods, a sandstone hill curves both northeastward and southeastward, leaving an amphitheater-like formation facing east. It forms a kind of windbreak so the natural and manmade fires that regularly consumed the surrounding prairie did not destroy the sheltered trees beyond. The dry prairie lies less than a mile south along this sandstone ridge.

Of singular value in Abraham's Woods — and one of the primary reasons for protection of this site — is the rich diversity of flora found here. Spring growth is especially splendid with woodland flowers and herbs in full bloom. Among the species that thrive in this woods are trillium species, trout lily, spring beauty, Dutchman's breeches and the rare annual, false mermaid *(Floerkia proserpinacoides)*. Another rare species, Goldie's fern *(Dryopteris goldiana)*, grows abundantly in the "amphitheater." With the passing of spring, the wood nettle and jewelweed prevail in the deep, cool forest understory.

Abraham's Woods is considered one of the most stable and self-sustaining communities of its type in southern Wisconsin and, as such, is an essential teaching and research laboratory for UW plant and forest scientists.

Protected: 40 Acres. Protection Goal: 150 Acres. Southern Wisconsin. Located in Green County 35 miles south of Madison. Owned and managed by the University of Wisconsin and used primarily for education. Contact the Director, UW-Arboretum, 1207 Seminole Hwy., Madison, WI 53713 or call (608) 262-2748 for more information on this preserve.

Brule River

Thick river-edge pines reflect their magnificence in the water against stirring sound effects from a wilderness sanctuary.

brown trout

One of the Conservancy's most ambitious projects in Wisconsin depends on the cooperation of many individuals. The Brule River Conservation Easement Program is intended to bring more than 5000 acres of one of the state's largest and highest quality forests under perpetual protection from destructive use. The white cedar and pine forests are particularly well developed here. Working with local landowners — many of whom have permanent or vacation residences on their property — the Conservancy secured conservation easements from the owners to preserve riverbank, swamp and forest along the Brule and the waterway itself. Under this voluntary program, private landowners agree to limit commercial development, construction, degradation of watercourses, off-road vehicle use, spraying, logging and mining, while continuing to use their land as a home site and for compatible recreation.

In this nine-mile stretch of a great northern river there are many of the "elements of natural diversity" that distinguish Conservancy projects. Rare and threatened plant and animal species thrive here. Nine major biotic communities are identified within the sphere of the river. Considered by some fishermen as one of the nation's top five trout fishing rivers, the Brule is pristine. This unique preserve encompasses nearly one-third of the river's length, the largest area of land within the Brule watershed that has escaped extensive and detrimental development.

The majestic upland pine forests dominate one's first impression of the Brule. The stands of old-growth red and white pines —

some individual specimens perhaps exceeding 300 years of age — are found nowhere else in the state. Wisconsin's largest single white pine grows here. The tall pines provide valuable nesting habitat for the imperilled bald eagle (*Haliaeetus leucocephalus*) and osprey (*Pandion haliaetus*), both of which hunt the Brule for fish.

Another significant community in this preserve is the lowland cedar swamp community, one of the best examples of its type left in the state. Here the colorful tall white bog orchid (*Habenaria dilatata*) grows with a wealth of other species in a richly diverse ecosystem.

The timber wolf (*Canus lupus*), an endangered species not now considered a permanent resident of Wisconsin, also inhabits the Brule River environment. Some 90 bird species are recorded in this nesting sanctuary, eleven of them considered rare in the state: black-backed woodpecker, three-toed woodpecker, yellow-bellied flycatcher, Swainson's thrush, ruby-crowned kinglet, Cape May warbler, red crossbill, evening grosbeak, Connecticut warbler, black-throated blue warbler and green heron. The diversity of life in this preserve even extends to the river's spawning beds for brown, rainbow and brook trout.

Conservancy involvement in the Brule River preserve began in 1979 with a biological analysis of the area. Negotiations with landowners began in 1981 and continue to the present.

Protected: 4,947 Acres. Protection Goal: 5,700 Acres. Northwestern Wisconsin. Located in Douglas County in the southern section of the Brule River State Forest, about 20 mi. east of Superior. The Nature Conservancy of Wisconsin administers a conservation easement program to protect ecologically sensitive areas from damaging development. All acreage is privately owned. Access is by permission of landowners ONLY or via boat on the river. Contact the Conservancy office at 1045 E. Dayton St., Rm. 209, Madison, WI 53703 for more information or call (608) 251-8140.

Flambeau River

A wilderness river twists and bends through the thick north woods, sanctuary to eagles and canoeists alike.

red squirrel

A remarkable warm-water river and forest ecosystem are preserved for all time in this expansive preserve. The Upper North Fork of the Flambeau River project encompasses approximately 300 feet on either side of a 12-mile stretch of the beautiful, free-flowing Flambeau. This stretch of the river is particularly valuable for its near-primitive condition as a virtually unpolluted river without a road-crossing or dam. Though the river was used for logging during the state's early history (old logging dam sites are still visible), the forest-covered riverbank and the river itself were not significantly marred by such industry. In fact, the land was purchased, in part, from industrial firms who recognized the importance of saving one of the finest natural river communities in the country.

Flambeau River contains a fine example of Wisconsin's legendary *boreal*, or far northern, forest — old-growth upland stands of white and red pines with an understory of white spruce, white cedar and balsam fir. This virgin forest contains trees that measure as much as two- to two-and-one-half feet in diameter. Their slow growth is an outcome of cold-climate conditions.

A variety of wetland communities are distributed along the length of the preserve, including a large tract of wetland conifer forest dominated by white cedar with ash, elm and red maple. Large silver maples along the river's edge are at the northern limit of their geographic range. A small spring-fed stream flows through this area, forming shallow ponds near the headwaters.

Endangered and threatened species thrive in this wilderness. It is a significant nesting/feeding habitat for both bald eagles and osprey, with great potential for increased productivity. Cooper's hawk and red-shouldered hawk also nest in the woods of the Flambeau. The unpolluted water of the river supports a diverse natural game-fish community, including lake sturgeon, a species on the decline in other locations throughout the United States. The rare sucker, river redhorse, ruffed grouse, coyote, otter, beaver and bear are among the wildlife inhabiting narrow reaches of the riverbank. An uncommon plant species in the Flambeau preserve is the small round-leaved orchis (*Orchis rotundifolia*).

Land for the Flambeau River preserve was originally purchased by the Conservancy in 1985 following more than six years of complex negotiations. It was then sold to the Wisconsin Department of Natural Resources with deed restrictions on development. The preserve is among the most natural recreation areas in the state for canoeing and fishing, and its biological diversity and ecological quality make it well-suited for research and education.

Protected: 1,060 Acres. Protection Goal: 1,800 Acres. Northern Wisconsin. Located in Ashland, Iron and Price Counties on upper north fork of river above the city of Park Falls. Owned and managed by the Wisconsin Department of Natural Resources (DNR) as a State Natural Area for research and recreation. For more information, contact the DNR at 101 S. Webster St., Madison, WI 53702 or call (608) 266-2277.

Jackson Harbor Ridges

northern harbor

An island beach stretches out into great Lake Michigan waves, elements of nature in harmony.

Protected: 39 Acres. Protection Goal: 90 Acres. Northeastern Wisconsin. Located in Door County on Washington Island. Owned by the Town of Washington and managed by the Washington Island Natural Area Board. Contact Arni Richter, Washington Island, WI 54246 for more information or call (414) 847-2296.

Jackson Harbor Ridges is a sheltered harbor facing northeast along the shoreline of Washington Island. It is a small preserve that features an outstanding collection of natural communities, including beach, lake dunes and ridges, calcareous sand flats and conifer forest. This rare combination of ecosystems that constitutes Jackson Harbor is the only beach of its kind known on the islands surrounding the Door Peninsula.

Fine boreal, or northern, plant types are present here due to the cool, moist climate. These include the rare dwarf lake iris *(Iris lacustris)* and arctic primrose *(Primula mistassinica).* The beach area undulates with areas of dry to wet sand and interdunal swales that rise west to a stand of pines. The site provides a magnificent view across the harbor. This wet, upland forest also contains white cedar, fir and spruce trees. Other plants identified among the Jackson Harbor dunes and ridges include shrubby St. John's-wort, sand coreopsis, prairie sandreed, northern comandra, stiff sandwort, dune goldenrod and a variety of sedges.

Protection of the Jackson Harbor Ridges was begun by the Town of Washington in 1973, with assistance from the Conservancy. Twenty-seven acres of this natural area are devoted to biological and wildlife study, photography and "careful walking."

Lulu Lake

Cattails and aquatic wildflowers accent the still lake that is a centerpiece of this vast expanse of Kettle Moraine beauty.

sandhill cranes

One of the state's finest wetland ecosystems is a cooperative effort of conservation easement and long-standing protection among The Nature Conservancy of Wisconsin, the Wisconsin Department of Natural Resources and private landowners. Conservancy acquisitions made in 1986 were given to the Wisconsin Department of Natural Resources for future management while the Conservancy maintains the easements. The DNR had made many earlier purchases for various conservation purposes. Lulu Lake glitters amidst the rich, marshy area in the upper reaches of the Mukwonago River. It is made up of diverse communities from river streams to oak openings. Portions of the preserve — notably a portion of the oak opening — are protected as a dedicated State Natural Area widely used for education and research.

Several significant natural communities at Lulu Lake are worthy of note: the high-quality lake, the calcareous fen and an increasingly rare oak opening. The 84-acre lake supports a sizable population of game fish such as bluegills and bass as well as species rare in Wisconsin, including long-eared sunfish (*Lepomis megalotis*) and star-head topminnow (*Fundulus nottii*). Surrounding wetlands include fen, sedge meadow, bog and shrub-carr. Some of the richest, undisturbed plant communities on the site contain the endangered tussock bullrush (*Scirpus cespitosus*) and rare swamp agrimony (*Agrimonia parviflora*), found at only one other site in the state. The endangered cricket frog (*Acris crepitans blachardi*) and state-threatened Blanding's turtle (*Emydoidea blandingi*) are some of the many animal species that take shelter in the Lulu Lake wetlands.

The upland communities, dominated by oak and hickory trees, represent the pre-settlement landscape of Wisconsin when more than five million acres of the state were oak opening. State-threatened species, northern kittentail (*Besseya bullii*) and Cooper's hawk (*Accipiter cooperii*), inhabit these uplands.

Management of Lulu Lake revolves around preventing damage to high-quality, rare natural features, as well as working to improve their quality and viability by essential intervention. The Conservancy does prescribed burning, road closure, fencing, brush clearing, weed removal and ecological monitoring. Compatible human activities allowed include research, education, fishing and nature study.

Protected: 495 Acres. Protection Goal: 2400 Acres (public & private land). Southeastern Wisconsin. Located in both Walworth and Waukesha Counties. A high-quality wetland ecosystem dedicated as a State Natural Area and of statewide scientific interest. Owned and managed by the Wisconsin Department of Natural Resources and private landowners. Contact the DNR at 101 S. Webster St., Madison, WI 53702 or call (608) 266-2277 for more information.

Michigan Island

Our north island legacy of lake beaches and hardwood forest survives against time and the timbering of Wisconsin's past.

island shore

Michigan Island is one of 22 Apostle Islands scattered in an archipelago off the northern coast of Wisconsin in Lake Superior. The beach front portion of the Michigan Island preserve belongs to a 520 square mile National Lakeshore area along the Bayfield Peninsula. Known today for their beauty and tourist appeal, the Islands and Lakeshore stand as living remnants of the Ice Age, featuring valuable examples of glacially Keweenawan sculptered sandstone, red clays and sand beaches. The Lake Superior sandstone was once the source of a booming late 19th-century industry in "brownstone," used for construction in the eastern and midwestern U.S.

Among existing landforms are small lakes formed by barrier beaches and a stretch of old-growth hemlock forest extending from an impressive lake beach. Like many of the other islands in the chain, the northern hardwood species on Michigan Island were heavily logged from early settlement days into the 1900s, but have recovered their forest aspect.

A sizable community of birds inhabits the island, including nesting colonials like the double-crested cormorant and the great blue heron. White-tailed deer, black bear, snowshoe hare, red fox and coyote roam the island. In the waters, lake trout, whitefish, herring and smelt are part of a teeming commercial and sport fishing industry.

The Conservancy has worked with the National Park Service since 1970 in helping to identify and preserve the scenic and biological resources of Michigan Island.

Protected: 1564 Acres. Protection Goal: 1564 Acres. Northern Wisconsin. Located in Ashland County off the northern coast of the state in Lake Superior. One of 21 islands in the Apostle Islands group belonging to the National Lakeshore. Owned and managed by the National Park Service. For more information contact Superintendent, National Park Service, Apostle Islands National Lakeshore, P.O. Box 729, Bayfield, WI 54814 or call (715) 779-3397.

Porcupine Lake Wilderness

The serenity of a crystalline lake evokes that sense of quiet isolation so magical in the deep northern woods.

beaver

Located in one of the few designated wilderness areas east of the Mississippi River, this four-acre tract lies on the eastern shore of Wisconsin's Porcupine Lake. The Nature Conservancy of Wisconsin purchased the tract in 1985 as an addition to the Porcupine Lake Wilderness area within the 844,604-acre Chequamegon National Forest. The land was then sold to the United States Forest Service and put under their wilderness designation.

Two communities of statewide significance are found here: a soft-water lake and northern mesic forest. The lake is of pristine quality and drains into Porcupine Creek. Northern pike, largemouth and smallmouth bass and panfish inhabit its waters. Mature upland trees and conifers dominate the lakeshore vegetation on this rugged tract. Small streams on the sloping ridges feed into the lake. Adjoining wetlands provide nesting habitat for ducks and other migratory fowl.

Though access to these remote wilds is only over rough trails or by boat, hiking, nature study and fishing are popular activities in this area.

Protected: 4 Acres by The Nature Conservancy, nearly 4000 acres by the United States Forest Service. Protection Goal: 4235 Acres. Northern Wisconsin. Located in Bayfield County within the Chequamegon National Forest. Owned and managed by the United States Forest Service. For more information, contact Superintendent, Chequamegon National Forest, 157 N. 5th Avenue, Park Falls, WI 54552 or call (715) 762-2461.

Renak-Polak Woods

snail

The forest primeval thrives within sight of the teeming city in this river-bend woods of old trees and abundant wildflowers.

Renak-Polak Woods combines several adjacent tracts of land that together represent one of the last southern mesic hardwood forests in Racine County and one of the best in the state. Large red oak, sugar maple, white ash and a fine stand of American beech trees help create the deep woods feeling engendered by this preserve. Such "old growth," or near-climax growth, is dominant at Renak-Polak, where a history of sparse logging has created a forest in various stages of succession.

Proximity to the Root River means this preserve is nestled in a setting of gently sloping ridges and broad valleys. A spring-fed pond on the site produces a stream that angles its way through much of the forest. The deep woods and stream combination encourage a wealth of plants. As many as 134 species are identified at Renak-Polak, including many spring ephemerals like hepatica, Dutchman's breeches, bloodroot, spring beauty and cardamine. Rare forest species of ginseng *(Panax quinquefolius)* and red trillium *(Trillium recurvatum)* are also found here.

The Conservancy originally acquired part of the preserve in 1971 through a combination of gifts and purchases. Ownership and management were then transferred to the University of Wisconsin-Parkside. Renak-Polak Woods is a Designated State Natural Area and significant site for education and research.

Protected: 112 Acres. Protection Goal: 160 Acres. Southeastern Wisconsin. Located in Racine County east of the Root River in Caledonia Township. Designated as a State Natural Area. Several tracts of maple-beech climax woods owned and managed by UW-Parkside. For more information, contact the Department of Life Sciences, UW-Parkside, Kenosha, WI 53140 or call (414) 553-2206.

Rush Creek Bluffs

Steep, prairie ridges afford a magnificent panoramic view of this Mississippi River landscape.

red-tailed hawk

A diverse and splendid collection of biological communities characterizes the Rush Creek Bluffs preserve as one of the most remarkable tracts of Wisconsin land that borders the Mississippi. More than two miles of limestone-capped bluffs face the river here, parted by crystal-clear Rush Creek as it empties into the larger muddy river's flow. The steep outcroppings are punctuated by dry prairie remnants known as "goat prairies." This site provides a rare example of the few remaining native hillside prairies left in the state. Prairie plants such as leadplant, big and little bluestem, blazingstar, wood betony, still goldenrod and bird's-foot violet are preserved season after season in this spot.

Upland hardwood forest thrives on the north- and east-facing slopes of the bluffs — red and white oak dominate with hickory, cottonwood, aspen, black walnut and elm. Groundcover of dogwood, hazelnut, woodland herbs and forbs trace the slopes beneath. In the bottomland along the creek, red and silver maple, river birch, willow and box elder are found. The red-shouldered hawk, a state-threatened species, nests in this "streambank" forest.

Rush Creek itself is a quality trout stream flowing northeast to southwest, fed by a host of springs and streams throughout the preserve. The ecological diversity of Rush Creek Bluffs attracts a variety of wildlife, including deer, grouse, raccoon, muskrat and beaver. Indian mounds and campsites have also been identified at the site.

Rush Creek Bluffs was acquired by the Conservancy in 1979, then transferred to the Wisconsin Department of Natural Resources for their protection. The preserve is a Dedicated State Natural Area.

Protected: 1,143 Acres. Protection Goal: 1600 Acres. Southwestern Wisconsin. Located in Crawford County on the banks of the Mississippi River, northwest of Ferryville. Dedicated as a State Natural Area. Owned and managed by the Wisconsin Department of Natural Resources. For more information, contact the DNR at 101 S. Webster St., Madison, WI 53702 or call (608) 266-2277.

Toft Point

Rocky shoreline to marshy lagoon, tall pines to forest flowers . . . all tell of undisturbed beauty in a precious place.

pine cone

Toft Point had been protected for generations by the careful foresight of the Toft family. The land was sold to the Conservancy in 1966, thereby achieving the family's longtime wish to preserve a uniquely natural part of Wisconsin. The Conservancy subsequently transferred ownership of Toft Point to the University of Wisconsin-Green Bay and it is now the site of study by many university classes and nature groups.

The value of Toft Point is its high-quality shoreline protected from the disruption of human activity. Ridges and swales rise along the southeast portion of the preserve, while a shallow lagoon distinguishes a marshy environment on the northeast shore. The upland area of Toft Point was once a boreal forest of tall northern trees. Cutting done more than 50 years ago transformed the forest habitat to white pine, white cedar, hemlock, black ash and balsam fir — growing abundant and mature. Growth now taking place is restoring the boreal character of the land. Forest birds such as the red-breasted nuthatch, winter wren and olive-sided flycatcher abound and the forest floor is home to some rare orchids (*Calypso bulbosa*) and other common but beautiful plants. Small-flowered grass-of-Parnassus is also found here and in only one other Wisconsin locale.

Protected: 633 Acres. Protection Goal: 800 Acres. Northeastern Wisconsin. Located in Door County along the Lake Michigan shore in Bailey's Harbor Township. Designated as a State Natural Area and a National Natural Landmark. Owned and managed by the University of Wisconsin-Green Bay. For more information, contact College of Environmental Studies, UW-Green Bay, 2420 Nicolet Dr., Green Bay, WI 54301 or call (414) 465-2371.

Other Protected Areas

The Wisconsin Nature Conservancy assisted in protecting these additional natural areas. As indicated here, many are now owned and managed by various other state and local agencies. Listings include location, acreage and contact agency. DESIGNATED State Natural Areas are marked with the initials **NA**. DEDICATED State Natural Areas are marked with a *. See p. 7 for explanation of *Designated* and *Dedicated*.

Ableman's Gorge — Sauk County, 16 Acres, University of Wisconsin-Madison, **NA**.

Alexander Prairie — Pierce County, 30 Acres, Joan & Richard Alexander.

Anderson Bottomlands — Iowa County, 119 Acres, University of Wisconsin-Madison.

Apple River Canyon — St. Croix County, 115 Acres, Wisconsin Department of Natural Resources, **NA**.

Bean Lake — Jefferson County, 88 Acres, Wisconsin Department of Natural Resources, **NA**.

Benedict Prairie — Kenosha County, 6 Acres, University of Wisconsin-Milwaukee.

Beulah Bog — Walworth County, 63 Acres, Wisconsin Department of Natural Resources, **NA**.

Big Rib River — Lincoln & Marathon Counties, 720 Acres, Wisconsin Department of Natural Resources.

Cactus Rock — Waupaca County, 20 Acres, Lawrence University, **NA**.

Carol Beach — Kenosha County, 5 Acres, Wisconsin Department of Natural Resources, *.

Cedarburg Bog — Ozaukee County, 23 Acres, University of Wisconsin-Milwaukee, **NA**.

Comstock Marsh — Marquette County, 265 Acres, Wisconsin Department of Natural Resources, **NA**.

Coolings Meadow — Waukesha County, 30 Acres, Waukesha County.

Fried-Sarona Woods — Washburn County, 159 Acres, University of Wisconsin-Eau Claire Foundation.

Fried-Sunfish Lake Forest — Washburn County, 69 Acres, University of Wisconsin-Eau Claire Foundation.

Genesee Oak Opening — Waukesha County, 52 Acres, Wisconsin Department of Natural Resources, **NA**.

Harris Tract — Kenosha County, 257 Acres, University of Wisconsin-Parkside.

Heritage Heights Sanctuary — Dane County, 9 Acres, Madison Parks Division.

High Trestle Woods — Winnebago County, 12 Acres, University of Wisconsin-Oshkosh.

Hixon Preserve/White River Fishery — Bayfield County, 392 Acres, Wisconsin Department of Natural Resources.

Holz Island — Waukesha County, 3 Acres, City of Muskego.

Honey Creek — Sauk County, 48 Acres, The Nature Conservancy, **NA**.

Hub City Bog — Richland County, 48 Acres, University of Wisconsin Regents, **NA**.

Ice Age Trail — Chippewa County, 160 Acres, Ice Age Park and Trail Foundation of Wisconsin, Inc.

Jung Hemlock Woods — Shawano County, 80 Acres, Wisconsin Department of Natural Resources, **NA**.

Kettle Pond — Dane County, 9 Acres, Madison Parks Division.

Lodde's Mill Bluff — Sauk County, 15 Acres, University of Wisconsin-Madison, **NA**.

Lower Wisconsin River State Forest — Dane, Grant, Iowa, Richland & Sauk Counties, 116 Acres, The Nature Conservancy.

Menard Isle — Lincoln County, 334 Acres, Wisconsin Department of Natural Resources.

Milwaukee Arboretum — Ozaukee County, 56 Acres, University of Wisconsin-Milwaukee.

John Muir Memorial Park — Marquette County, 27 Acres, Marquette County, *.

Muralt Bluff Prairie — Green County, 13 Acres, Green County, **NA**.

Namekagan Preserve — Bayfield County, 40 Acres, Cable Natural History Museum.

Newark Road Prairie — Rock County, 33 Acres, Beloit College, **NA**.

Oliver Prairie — Green County, 4 Acres, University of Wisconsin-Madison, **NA**.

Sigurd F. Olson Memorial Forest — Burnett County, 183 Acres, Northland College.

Otsego Marsh Preserve — Columbia County, 39 Acres, Goose Pond Sanctuary.

Peat Lake — Kenosha County, 171 Acres, Wisconsin Department of Natural Resources.

Pike River — Marinette County, 37 Acres, Wisconsin Department of Natural Resources.

Pine and Popple Wild Rivers — Florence County, 40 Acres, Wisconsin Department of Natural Resources.

Puchyan Prairie — Green Lake County, 120 Acres, Wisconsin Department of Natural Resources, **NA**.

Ranger Mac Fen — Racine County, 33 Acres, University of Wisconsin-Parkside.

Ridges Sanctuary — Door County, 126 Acres, The Ridges Sanctuary, **NA.**

Rush River Delta — Pierce County, 119 Acres, Wisconsin Department of Natural Resources, **NA.**

Schmidt Maple Woods — Clark County, 86 Acres, University of Wisconsin-Eau Claire Foundation, **NA.**

Sheboygan Memorial Arboretum — Sheboygan County, 34 Acres, University of Wisconsin-Sheboygan.

Squaw Bay — Bayfield County, 12 Acres, The Nature Conservancy.

St. Croix Island Wildlife Area — St. Croix County, 80 Acres, Wisconsin Department of Natural Resources.

Two Creeks Buried Forest — Manitowoc County, 12 Acres, Wisconsin Department of Natural Resources, **NA.**

UW-Arboretum Additions — Dane County, 13 Acres, University of Wisconsin-Madison.

UW-Milwaukee Field Station — Ozaukee County, 103 Acres, University of Wisconsin-Milwaukee.

West Shore Wildlands — Brown County, 400 Acres, Brown County.

Whitefish Dunes State Park — Door County, 80 Acres, Wisconsin Department of Natural Resources.

Index

8/9/8